<u>Logic</u> <u>Behind</u> <u>Religion</u>

Religion of Abraham

Don B. Bandari, MD

Gotham Books

30 N Gould St.
Ste. 20820, Sheridan, WY 82801
https://gothambooksinc.com/

Phone: 1 (307) 464-7800

© 2023 *Don B. Bandari*. All rights reserved.

No part of this book may be reproduced, stored in a retrieval system, or transmitted by any means without the written permission of the author.

Published by Gotham Books (March 17, 2023)

ISBN: 979-8-88775-240-2 (P)

ISBN: 979-8-88775-241-9 (E)

Because of the dynamic nature of the Internet, any web addresses or links contained in this book may have changed since publication and may no longer be valid.

The views expressed in this work are solely those of the author and do not necessarily reflect the views of the publisher, and the publisher hereby disclaims any responsibility for them.

Table of Contents

Preface	1
Chapter 1	7
Does Gd Exist?	7
Chapter 2	13
Religion And The Religious	13
Chapter 3	21
A True Religion	21
Chapter 4	31
Conversion	31
Chapter 5	37
A Mixture Of Religions	37
Chapter 6	45
True Faith	45
Chapter 7	55
Unity And Differences	55
Chapter 8	64
Conclusion	64

To my intelligent wife
To my kind mother
And
In memory of my father

Preface

Before I begin, I need to thank Gd for giving me the opportunity, the power, and the patience to do a small thing by writing this book.

Throughout my research, I tried hard to follow, as a true believer would, each of the religions I have studied and not judge any of them through the eyes of my previous beliefs.

I started forming this concept of religions when I was very young, maybe in the fifth or sixth grade, and by the age of fifteen, I began to write down my thoughts and whatever information I could gather from the religions I studied. I originally started writing this book in 1989, when I was in medical school. When I finished medial school, I finished writing it. Again, for many years, I thought about the concepts in this book and made sure they matched the ideologies of the religions I studied. I am proud to say that none of the concepts I wrote about twelve or thirteen years ago has changed. This is almost 100 percent the same book I wrote when I was in school and school.

The reason for my pride is that writing this kind of book required a pure heart to see things as they are. In our time, and even a long time before our time, the concept of the differences among religions has occupied many minds in a search for the solution to the problem of religion. Many books try to defend or disprove one religion or another. If you read these books carefully, you will find that many of the facts in them are not even proved to themselves. Almost all these books take a small and complicated concept of the religion, discuss it in detail, and then form conclusions in such a way that no doubt can remain in the mind of anyone who reads the book. The result of this kind of book and this kind of ideology is the war between religions.

The followers of the religions who read these kinds of books start to love their religion and make fun of the faithful of other religions. This is a difficult concept for the followers to understand. On the other hand, the human mind has the capability to solve almost all of man's problems. The question is, why has this problem continued in civilization for thousands of years? The answer is that religion works with our emotions and our minds. It is easier to change your mind or convince someone to follow your way of thinking than it is to change an emotion toward something. When we grow up, we automatically tend to accept whatever ideology has been placed in our life until we die. Very few people try to find a better way of thinking and living. The attraction to the ideologies around us can be so strong that almost no changes are expected in civilization in the end. However, civilization will find its own way. The question then becomes one of whether civilization is going in the right direction. Here again, you will find groups who do not like one kind of civilization, and the fighting will start.

In between are other ideas that occur in the small but pure minds of individuals who stay silent. These ideas die with them. This book is simply an idea that came to my mind. I believe this idea covers not only most of our difficulty in the perception of the religions but also the differences between the religions—and finally, the right path of living, called the religion of Abraham.

This is not the only way, nor is it the end of any research. It is just the beginning. The problem is that, unfortunately, through thousands of years of human civilization, the human mind has been under so much pressure and sometimes negligence that religion has become like an archaeological discovery. It is difficult to go back and find the origin of any ideology or religion that came to humanity and to inquire how it has changed or taken another road. If someone wishes to find the right path, he should spend many years in study, and at the end, he might or might not get there. You can see in human history that many philosophers have tried to bring new ideologies to the world. Many of them could not survive at the beginning, and many that did later had to leave. What we have now is almost nothing enthusiastic in the concept of religion.

The only strong concept in religion is the concept of faith. Belief in religion is still strong among many people of the world because it has brought a lot of comfort to many, and no one can challenge the past. The concept is that, human beings need Gd for their growth and for their everyday living. Gd tells the people how they should live. Gd gives them their reward and punishment.

For me, the reasons for Gd were not a major issue to begin with. I could see that if I did not believe in Gd, there would be no reason to spend my time trying to find the best way to live. The best way of living, would be just enjoying life. I know that many people do not need this reason to follow Gd in their lives. But, for me, from the beginning, I needed someone above me who could see me all the time, return to me, and know that I could return to him at some time. I am not just talking about reward and punishment. The concept of Gd is much broader than that. The concept of Gd is having someone who supervises everything in the world, someone who gives value to humanity and good deeds. Because of Him, it is worth to sacrifice, the most valuable items in life, for the sake of making someone else happy. This is the concept of love, of having someone who loves you truly.

The concept of Gd was not so hard for me to understand. What was difficult to understand was the concept of religion. I see people of different religions who believe in their own so much that they cannot tolerate any other. Because of this, they are ready to fight and even sacrifice their own lives for their religions. How can anyone be so sure about his religion? I can understand that religion is also a kind of faith that does not need much reason, but when we are talking about religion, we are not talking about just one. How can we pick one, have faith in it, and reject all others? The pain gets deeper when you see so many books by the doctors and philosophers of these religions, written in such a way that you begin to think the religions are at such odds and in such contradiction that there is no way other than fighting.

Many books that are considered well researched give an overall view on a particular religion. Even though they seem right but the research is not complete, and there is a lot of doubt in them. Interestingly, the conclusions in these books are written in such ways that leave no doubt in the reader's mind.

Research on material dealing with human belief and culture needs a specific kind of setting. In his book, which talks about different cultures and different customs from about one thousand years ago, Abu Raihan Al-Biruni, one of the biggest Eastern scientists and historians, points out this fact nicely (reference 1):

And this object cannot be obtained by way of reasoning from philosophical concepts, nor from induction based upon the observations of our senses. It comes solely by absorbing the information of those who have written a tradition, of the members of different religions, and of adherents of the different doctrines and religious sects, by whom the institutions we are interested in are used. And it comes by making their opinions a basis on which afterwards to build up an understanding of their system; in addition, we must compare their traditions and opinions among themselves, when we try to establish such a system. But before that, we must clear our minds from all those accidental circumstances that deprave most men, from all causes which are liable to make people blind against the truth. For example, inveterate custom, party spirit, rivalry, being addicted to one's passions, the desire to gain influence, etc. For that which I have mentioned, is the nearest way you could take, that leads to true end, and the most efficient help towards removing all the clouds of uncertainty and doubt, which beset the subject. It is impossible in any other way to reach the same purpose, notwithstanding the greatest care and exertion.

His book was an inspiration for me to make the effort to find the truth. Unfortunately, throughout my research, I could not find another book like this one.

The other problem we face is that scientists and researchers have made the problem of religion a philosophical and highly educated matter. I am not against philosophy, but I do not think it is a philosophical matter. The problem with philosophy and logic is that any philosophical reason can be disputed in the future, and anything we think is already proved can be disproved eventually. We cannot make religion a philosophical idea, because any philosophical ideology is subject to improvement and change. Religion is a faith that needs to stay in the mind of humanity.

Philosophy has a role in religion in the same way that other sciences do. It must be that a combination of religion and human knowledge can make a better life for humanity.

The problem I see related to the researchers and the authorities of the religions is that they never try to remove all the doubts from the human mind. A true faith needs to be without doubt. There are two ways to remove doubt. The first is to forget about it and just focus on what we know. This results in a kind of faith that is based on lack of knowledge; unfortunately, this is the kind of faith we see in our culture.

There is another way, and I think this is healthier: we must not forget doubt but acknowledge it and try to answer it as much as we can. In this way, we are always in a state of searching and researching. At the same time, we are improving and moving to a higher degree that has less doubt in it. Of course, we cannot answer all questions, because we do not have enough knowledge, but acknowledging doubt makes us think and research, also making us respect whatever information we gather through any sources. This way, we can be sure we are on the right track, because we are always checking our shortages and finding the solutions for them. The only way to go straight on any pathway is to think about the probabilities of going wrong and making mistakes—the same concepts you can see in the problem of Gd and understanding him.

Many philosophers try to disprove Gd. Because they think the reasons are not sufficient to prove Gd, they go ahead and say there is no proof for Him. So if there is no proof, no one can be obligated to follow Him. The mistake they make is that such a philosophy not only does not solve our problems but also creates more doubt. You can see that no one can be sure if Gd exists. On the other hand, many people feel they need Gd to pray to for help or even just to cry to. People see that philosophy is not going to get them anywhere. They feel the need for Gd to help and live with.

This combination of feelings, logic, and a wandering mind causes people more confusion.

A simple solution for this problem is that philosopher and thinker both need to understand that if they cannot prove Gd' existence at this time, it does not mean that He cannot be proven in the future. The problem of Gd may be more easily solved in the future, and He yet may be proven to humanity. The problem is what we should do until that time. Should we set aside Gd and chase after other things, or should we keep the concept of Gd in the corner, not forgetting him but not doing anything with Him either? The other option is to turn inward, into our strong feelings for Gd, and at the same time, try to obtain more information and understand Him better.

At any rate, this book is not meant to prove or disprove Gd. But when it comes to the problem of religions, this book speaks loudly. After we accept the concept of Gd, accepting the religions will automatically come to mind because if there is a Gd, there should be a relationship with Him. That relationship comes through religion. In this book, we will discuss this concept in great detail.

I tried to structure this book in a basic fashion and think about all the possibilities and all the questions, gradually building a theory to find a solution to the problem of religions. I will not make any exaggerations about this book, and I should emphasize that not all the concepts of this book are necessarily right. I studied nearly all the religions and came up with a conclusion that does not contradict the basic concept of religions. This is just the beginning. There is probably a long way to go.

In each chapter of this book, I bring up a few fundamental questions and try to answer them, gradually building up to a concept that leads us to more questions and, eventually, to a simple conclusion. You may find that some concepts of this book are on the edge and not easy for you to accept. The concepts in this book are connected to each other like a chain, each one supporting the other. On the other hand, maybe everything in this book is wrong; perhaps the conclusions are not right. If this is the case, and someone can prove it to me, I promise that I will be the first to put this book away and search for a new theory that can answer the questions.

These questions have been in our minds for thousands of years and have caused wars and distrust among different nations and religions. This is the time to find the solution. Even if this book does not answer all the questions and the conclusions are not right, I think what it can do is open the pathway to more research. I worked very hard to avoid any prejudgments and previous belief or disbelief of any religion or ideology. I almost disintegrated my own religion in an effort to understand every concept of other religions. I hope those who read this book will realize the simplicity and the purity of the discussions.

In each chapter and for each of the concepts that I needed to find references for, I only referred to those authorities of the religions that have acceptance by their followers. I just quoted the words from their books without any interpretation. As I have said, the references are not many, because most of the books written in this matter are not following the right path of research. For some of the concepts of the religions, I simply relied on general public opinion about religion because I did not think they needed any references. For example, Buddhism is not a religion that has come from Gd; it does not discuss the concept of Gd to begin with.

I tried to stick with the basics and avoid complicated and complex discussions. I did not go into detail too often, because the discussions would be very long, making it hard to find any conclusion. The second reason is that I believe many concepts of religion are like other problems in daily life: a simple problem becomes a major issue because we did not want to deal with it in the beginning. I try to build a fundamental knowledge; anything more than this is up to the individual to find out for himself and get the information he needs. If an individual does not agree with any part of the discussion, he should discuss the issue in a healthy and genuine way to find the right answers. There is a solution to our problems in this world. The ultimate answer in this world will come from Gd. The only responsibility we have as followers of Gd is to find the best pathway to reach Him and try to unite. At the same time, each individual can go further to satisfy his heart and mind.

At the end, I want to thank Gd again. I hope people find this book a service to the human mind. Certainly, this is just the beginning of a new way of thinking, and we need His help more and more now. People should also be ready to compromise and sacrifice daily working lives to find the better way of living. The path is hard and the road is difficult, but with our own efforts and the help of Gd, one day we will achieve what we wish for now.

Sincerely,

Don B. Bandari, MD

Reference:

1. Athar-ul-Bakiya, The Chronology of Ancient Nations, by Al-Biruni, translated by C. Edward Sachau. William H. Allen and Co., London, 1879, preface page 3.

Chapter 1
DOES GD EXIST?

Does Gd really exist? Do we have enough evidence of the existence of Gd? What is Gd, exactly? What is the relation between Gd and us? Before approaching and discussing religion, we should know all manners of religions.

Many published books have tried to prove or disprove the existence of Gd. Some are philosophical, some are scientific, and some come from people's emotions about Gd. Many philosophers have written so deeply that reading and understanding them is sometimes extremely difficult. Some people are easily convinced of the existence of Gd; they simply pray night and day and are happy with that. On the other hand, there are those who will not be convinced in any way to believe in Gd. Who is wrong—those who believe in Gd… or those who do not?

I believe that Gd exists. However, I am not going to talk about the existence of Gd in this book. I am not even sure there are enough reasons, logical or scientific, to prove the existence of Gd. But my belief in Gd is the reason I have written this book. I think that when Gd says, "I am the Gd who created you and brought you into this world" or when He says, "I am the creator of the whole universe," that is enough. To my way of thinking, something created the world. I might not understand the nature of HIM completely but my mind understands and comprehends the concept of Gd because He is not just a creator to me; Gd is everything. He is the goal of the world. He is the beginning and the end. He is hope. He is the one that everyone should look for and try to reach. Gd has value and is valuable to the world. Without Him, there is no value. Nothing lasts forever.

How can you give value to something or someone that you know is not going to continue? We don't know when, but we know that it is not going to last forever. If something is not going to be here forever, no matter how much value we place upon it, it will lose that value someday. So, for me, acceptance of Gd is not so hard. Not that I understand Him, or even think I can understand Him, but he gives value to my life, and I am looking for this value. This is not a philosophical or scientific reason. It is a simple reason, which can find its way to the hearts of simple people, and it is the greatest honor to be a simple man or woman.

The problem is that if we do not believe in Gd, we cannot say for sure what is good and what is not good. What is good now might not be good in a few years. We know that many formerly good things from a few decades or centuries ago are not good anymore. So, whatever we have is relative. Because the goodness depends on what we see it, right now, we cannot say for sure what is good and what is not. I believe that Gd is the one who enlightens the world and shows us what is good and what is not good. In other words, our existence completely depends on His existence. He is the one who gives meaning to life. Without Him, we would be like the blind, with far to go and no direction. We can say that we don't even know ourselves fully and have to know humanity before we get to Gd. We have a long, long way to go.

The problem is that we do not know why we are here and what comes after. Will we go on after death? Is death the end of everything? If we are looking for the answers to our lives, we have to know Gd. As I said before, the purpose of this book is not to prove or disprove the existence of Gd. This book will deal mostly with religions. The reason I started this chapter with Gd is to have a base for our discussion in the next chapters because religions are based on the existence of Gd. And for many of us, dealing with the problem of religions starts with the understanding of the essence of Gd.

I believe faith in Gd does not need reason, logic, or scientific evidence. If faith were dependent on these things, we could not say that people in the past had enough faith, and faith would be dependent upon materialistic things that change continuously. The path to Gd is through our hearts, not through our minds. If the mind poses the hardest questions for proving or disproving Gd, the ultimate answers will come through the heart.

One of the problems the mind has, especially as far as an understanding of Gd, is that it cannot comprehend something that does not have any physical component. Gd does not have any physical component and is not sensible. Our minds not only cannot prove the existence of Gd but also cannot comprehend such a large power in the world. That is the reason that those philosophers who do not believe in Gd, instead of bringing their own reasons to disprove Gd, always come with the reasons to deny and disprove the reasons of those who do believe in Him. Their job is to prove that we do not have enough reason to believe in Gd. I believe that this is one the biggest mistakes in the history of the human mind.

As I will discuss in the next chapters, doubt is one of the most essential parts of the human mind. We live with doubt. Doubt is the basis of faith, and because of doubt, we think and grow up. Doubt in Gd should not be the reason that we do not believe in Gd. We should stay doubtful but search for answers more and more. Our job is to grow up and get to a level where we have less and less doubt; this will not happen unless we think about all the possibilities. One of the biggest possibilities in the world is Gd. We have to know Him. We really have to think about Him, and we cannot put Him aside unless we have enough knowledge about the origin or the end of the world. As long as we have these questions in our minds, there will always be Gd, and Gd is the answer for the old questions. I believe that as long as the life of human beings goes on, the doubt will always be with us and push us to that which we call Gd.

I believe that those who do not believe in Gd are in much greater doubt about themselves. They do not know what they are doing in this world or in their lives, and it might someday be proven that they are completely wrong. This doubt is dangerous because it is destructive. They are living in darkness, and one day they will regret it because it is based on lack of knowledge. What they say is that they don't know and don't want to know, and in my belief, this is wrong.

To me, the main proof of Gd is our need for Him. We can sense that without such a greater power, our own small power won't last. Our life won't have any meaning without Him. Whatever we do in this life won't have any consequence. The consequence of everything is going to be death. There is a way of living and there is a way of death, and I believe that the way of Gd is the way of living.

We should all ask ourselves what life is. What is the purpose of life? What is the role of humanity in this life? How should we live? What should we wait for? We are born, grow up, grow old, and die. Is that not what will happen to everyone? What I said is that if we are looking for answers, we should believe that something controls this world—and that controller is Gd. Gd does not do anything without purpose. Whatever He does, there is a reason behind it. If we are alive, if there is creation, there must be a reason behind it. You might not understand that reason, but because of belief in Gd, we find hope that there is a reason after all. One day we might find out that reason. But until that time, we have religion that says He created us and is our master. Religion is the relationship between Gd and humanity, creator and creature.

In summary, we might not know the reason behind creation, but when we believe in Gd, we can believe and hope that there is a reason behind it, though we cannot see it right now.

Our hearts can accept Gd, and our minds cannot rule out the existence of Gd. Our hearts tell us that there is Gd, that He created all good things in this world, and that

He is the one who gives meaning to the good things in this world. He is the one who tells us that if we go through hardship and suffering, someone will somehow know it in the end, and we will be rewarded. What we go through is not going to be for nothing, even though we might not get what we want. In other words, belief in Gd is something that goes through the heart, and more than anything else, our hearts tell us whether we should or should not believe in Gd. Maybe this is a personal thing for anyone who believes in Gd—or not.

In this book, what I am trying to say is that Gd is in our hearts. And this book is for those who believe in Gd and believe there is a reason behind creation. There is a reason that we live and die, and there is a reason for everything in this world.

Again, the goal behind this chapter and this book is not to prove the existence of Gd. If you need a book to prove the existence of Gd, you can easily obtain many others. Essentially, there is no proof that can 100 percent prove the existence of Gd. The belief in the existence of Gd is faith, but what I want to say is that belief in Gd can remove the doubt from our hearts. Even if, those who say we are in doubt might be right, but they forget that our doubt is what makes us good people, makes us people who do good things in this world. On the other hand, those who do not believe in Gd also have doubt about what they say and do, and I believe their doubt is worse than ours. Our doubts take us to construction, and their doubts take them to destruction. Our doubts lead us to believe in good, and their doubts lead them to believe in nothingness. We might not get to the point where we believe in Gd 100 percent, but we have a doubtful feeling that makes us believe and do good things, and I think this is a good belief.

Although we don't exactly know Gd, I believe that there are a few points we should know before we continue. During human history, many religions have thought that they believe in Gd; many religions have been made up that all teaching the concept of Gd. How can we know which religion is a true one? There are a few points we have to make clear in our minds before we continue. There are many questions that we cannot answer because we don't understand Gd completely. How is He? What is He? How did He come to us? These questions are mostly philosophical and are not going to be answered now, nor maybe ever, but there are a few basic points in understanding Gd, which I believe that anyone who does believe in Gd will truly understand them. With these few facts, we can simply recognize those religions that truly keep Gd as their basis and go after the right concept of Him.

We cannot claim that we know Gd. We cannot claim that we even understand a small particle of Him, and I think that is the definition of Gd, that Gd is beyond our understanding. Gd is not materialistic, and by itself, this means that He should not be limited to any place or time. It is simple to understand if something can be limited to a place; there is always going to be something bigger than him. There should not be anything bigger than Gd, and he should not be placed anywhere. If He is limited to time, then there should be some time that he did not exist, and by definition, that cannot be Gd. He should not have any limits. It should be all of everything, and everything should be included in Him. It is hard to understand, but that is what our minds tell us about who we should pray to. So if you want to understand Gd, the first step is to take him out of materialistic thinking.

In the next chapter, we will discuss the fact that any religion that believes in Gd in such a way—that He is not limited to anything, and that He is the only master in this world—is the kind of religion that truly believes in Gd. That kind of religion can be included in all discussions from now on. Any other religions that believe there is more than one Gd, or that there is a shape or time, or in any way think they can see him, feel him, or go to him are out of our discussion. In other words, I do not think those kinds of religions can give us a true and right knowledge of Gd.

I believe that most religions, at least at the present time, believe in Gd as an unlimited thing. They might not be fully right, but many of the religions we currently know believe that Gd is something that is not limited and is not of the material world. A complete philosophical and logical discussion about Gd is out of our discussion and is not an easy thing to go through. I can say that we should not be surprised that throughout history, many religions have made many mistakes about Gd because it is hard to understand Him. But these mistakes do not prove that the basics of the religion were wrong; they just tell us that the understanding of humanity has been wrong throughout history.

In all religions that believe in Gd, the ultimate goal of humanity is to understand Him. Through understanding Gd, human beings develop and their spirits go higher and higher, to a point that the only thing that matters is Gd—to please Gd and to be a part of Him as the source of all good in the world. As you can imagine, this is not an easy task to understand and to follow.

In summary, in my opinion, the ultimate goal of humanity is to understand and to know Gd truly. If we can do this, we will not need any religion, philosophy, or any other tools to achieve true life and true happiness. But how is it possible to know Gd? The answer is that there is a path to get to Him. We have to travel this path gradually to get to the point where we feel that we know and can change our lives accordingly. What I call this path is religion. We have to know the right path, and we have to know the right religion. If we find the right religion, the right path, we are going to reach the goal. If we take the wrong path, we will go the other way.

Some people believe that religions are nothing more than the production of the human minds plus knowledge plus all the experience of the human beings in the past. All these things can make a religion that shows them the right path to the right goal. In this book, I try to analyze most of these opinions. There are other opinions about religion that we will also discuss. My goal in this book is to get to a point that we can certainly say we are on the right path, even though we can never that say that we are totally right, or that we got to the point we wanted. The human mind continues to grow, understand, and find new things. I think we probably will not get to a point where we can say for sure that we are right, but we should try to get to a point where we can assure ourselves that we are on the right path, and if we continue, one day we will hopefully get to the ultimate light of Gd.

This book is based on belief in Gd, and after having this belief, we can continue and analyze different religions and different thoughts about Gd, but proving the existence of Gd is not the goal of this book. What I hope to accomplish in this book is to bring the different questions that can come to our minds and try to answer them. We cannot put away all the doubts in our minds, but we can get to the point where we can say we are on the right track.

We have thus far discussed that there is a Gd in this world and that religions exist. These questions will come in the next chapter: Which of these religions are true and which are not true? What are the criteria for being a true religion? As I finish this chapter, I pray to Gd again that He gives us the power to continue on His way.

Chapter 2
RELIGION AND THE RELIGIOUS

What is a religion? Is there any true religion in this world? What is the reason behind religion? Can we believe in Gd without religion? Does religion help us have better lives?

These are the main questions that have always been in the mind of man. Before we go into more detail, we have to answer them. Currently, few countries keep their religion part of politics. Most of us nowadays believe that religion should be a private thing that we discuss at home with the children. Most people in the world think about their religion after the everyday issues have been solved. Religion is secondary thing to all the other problems in life.

Most people do not have a profound or deep insight into religion. Even most philosophers and thinkers look at religion as an archeological remnant. Few have come to religion and looked at the depth of the religion to find the main purpose and effect of it.

It is difficult to say who or what is right in this world, as I said before, but there is one thing that surely is right. Religion should be a relationship between a human being and his Gd. If a religion is not a connection between a human being and Gd, I do not like to call it a religion. We can call it an ideology or anything else, but religion should be a connection between a human being and Gd. By this definition, many religions are going to be out of our discussion because many of these religions are not based on a connection between man and Gd. Few religions try to make this connection. Although some might be false religions, as long as a religion believes in Gd, it is going to be called a religion in this book.

At any rate, my definition of a religion is one that has kept its relationship with Gd. So first we have to see whether there is any religion that has kept its connection to Gd.

Many scientists believe that what we have today as religions are remnants of a collection of customs and prayers that have been collected over many years. Other scientists believe that a kind of religion in the past started with a prophet, but through the years has been changed so profoundly that what we have now is not even close to what it was in the past.

But on the other hand, you can see a few groups that look at religion differently. They view religion as something that gives them a goal and purpose in this world. They live by their religions, and everything comes from their religions. For them, religion gives them bravery, kindness, and life. Although they cannot answer philosophical and scientific questions, they can feel their religion inside them.

To me, the best cause for religion comes from the heart of religious people. A pure heart can answer questions better than the best scientist and the best philosopher can.

Let us review what we have discussed so far. I said that I believe in Gd as a starting point. Now, after a belief in Gd, the question is religion. We said that religion is the connection between Gd and humanity. If we believe in Gd, then we should believe in a connection between humanity and Gd, and we call that connection a religion. This connection should be from both sides. This connection should have started from Gd and should end with humanity. It is not our responsibility to go after religion because religion is a special path which starts from above. Gd is the creator, and if He created us and wanted us to seek and follow Him, He should have left us some tools to find Him. In other words, it is the responsibility of Gd to give us a clear path to find Him. He could not simply tell people to go find Him. Of course, it is our responsibility to grow and obtain enough knowledge so we can understand Gd as much as possible, but He would not want to leave the children at school without a book.

If we are the children and Gd is the principal of the school, there should be a connection between the principal and the children, like teachers or books. The teachers and books are religion. Again, it would be the responsibility of the principal to give the students the right books and the right teachers. After he does so, he can test the students to find out if they learned or not. If there is no book and no teacher, how can anybody expect the student to learn? Besides, I believe that the relationship between humanity and Gd is much deeper than any other relationship. In other relationships, we can feel, see, and find the right track, but between Gd and us, the relationship is much more complicated. We believe in somebody or something that is the source of goodness in this world; this is all that we know from Gd. We do not have any more knowledge about Gd besides what He himself has given us. Therefore, we believe that if there is a Gd and if there is humanity, if there is a creation and Gd created us, he should have created a path from humanity to Him, and that path is called religion.

If we believe in Gd, humanity, creation, and religion, then for all the generations, there should be at least one path that is completely safe and completely free of any doubt. Human beings should be able to rely on it and walk on that path. As we said, this is the responsibility of the creator. We as the creatures have the responsibility to find the creator, but the creator has the responsibility to keep at least one clear path for humanity to find Him, because he has the power to do so. Of course, it does not mean there cannot be more than one path or religion. At this point, we are not trying to find the right religion. The only thing we need is a clear path that came from Gd and has been saved through generations. Gd has spoken to human beings through the prophets, and the collection of his words has been saved in a few books that people believe have come from Gd.

What we need is a book we can rely on and can say for sure has the word of Gd without changes. It means we cannot accept even one small change through the whole book. This book should have a historical approval, meaning that by searching history and other archeological research, we should come to believe that the book is the same book that came from the prophets. I do not want to say historical research is the right way, but because we are examining a strong belief system, we need all our tools. It means the book we choose should have approval from both the sciences and faith.

I do not believe that the historical research that has been done so far has come to a true conclusion that we can rely on it. But on the other hand, I cannot just put all of it aside and say that I do not want to talk about it at all.

The only book that most researchers believe is the same book through generations, from the time of prophets to the present time, is the Koran. Almost all researchers believe that the book has not changed since the time of the prophets. I am not talking about the religion of Islam at this point. I am only referring to the book, and of course, the book and religion are two different things, which we will discuss later on.

We have to cover one more point. Belief that a book has come from Gd is totally a matter of faith. Like belief in Gd, belief in a book from Gd also requires faith. Everyone has to read the book for himself and make up his own mind. The same thing that we say about Gd is true of the books also. I do not think there is any way to prove whether any books have come from Gd. What we are discussing here is just scientific research that shows the book is the same book that has been through the generations from the time of the prophet. As I said, the basic concept consists of two parts: the belief in Gd and the belief that there is a relationship between Gd and us. If we believe in Gd, we should believe in a kind of message from Gd to humanity.

About the Koran, as mentioned, almost all researchers believe it is the same book that came from the prophets. Of course, some books say that it has been changed through the generations, but there is no historical remark about the changes in the Koran. I can refer you to a book that was written by the distinguished authorities in Islam, like Khoie. In his book *Al-Bayan*, he states that there have been doubts about changes in the Koran even between Muslims (although he disproves them). You can find the same thing in *Majma al-Bayan*, by Al-Sheikh Abu Ali al-Tabarsi. But altogether, no one has enough proof to say that Koran has been changed from the time of the prophets. Other non-Muslim scientists that have performed research on the origin of the Koran have concluded the same thing (reference 1).

Again, I have to emphasize that I'm not trying to prove that the Koran is a book that came from Gd. This is up to any individual to decide for himself. What I want to convey is the fact that we need a book that has the words of Gd. Both scientific and nonscientific researches should lead us to approve one book that has not been changed throughout time and to generate a strong belief in an existing path to Gd. As for these criteria, no book except the Koran qualifies. We are going to use the Koran as a key to understanding the concept of other religions.

If there was no book that both science and faith would approve, we could say, that there is not any religion in the world that we can trust and devote our lives to it. You can imagine that it is such an important concept that we have a book that we can say for sure has the words of the prophets. We can say at this point that at least one religion is alive. This concept about the Koran might provoke a number of discussions about other books, and I can imagine that it might have surprised many people, but this is purely scientific research, and there is not any other book in the world that has qualified based on the two criteria of faith and science.

At this point, I am not trying to prove or disprove any religion. We showed there is one connection alive between Gd and humanity. At least one path clearly establishes a relationship between Gd and humanity. In a future discussion, we can see how this relationship can prove or disprove the religions that exist.

What we've discussed so far is probably sufficient for those who believe in religion. For other people who do not see any benefit in observing religion, this discussion cannot satisfy them. Many philosophers do not see any benefit from religion and actually believe that religion is harmful for civilization.

So, our discussion has different aspects: first, whether there should be religion; second, whether any religion exists or not; third, whether the world benefits from religion? fourth aspect is whether this religion is the same one Gd wanted for humanity, and the last aspect is whether humanity is obligated to obey their religions.

I would like to start with the last question. Is humanity obligated to obey religion? I feel that the answer is yes. If we believe in Gd, we should believe that Gd wants us to live in a certain way. That way is what we call religion. I think this part is a matter of faith. If we have faith in Gd, somehow, we should have faith in religion too. Gd and religion are connected. The way of Gd is religion. So, if we want to be in the way of Gd, we should keep religion too.

Now let us go to this question: what is the benefit of observing the religion? Before we discuss this subject, I want to emphasize one point: even if we do not find any benefit to religion, it cannot disprove the importance of it in the world. As we said, religion is faith. When we believe in Gd, we believe in a power that is not of this materialistic world, and when we believe in religion, we continue to believe this. The belief that there are things that our minds cannot fully understand is the reason to believe in Gd and religion. We think that what Gd wants for us is the best, so if we believe in Gd, we should believe in religion too. We cannot say any more about the benefit of religion, because religion is the continuation of believing in Gd. Again, whether we find it beneficial or not, it cannot prove or disprove religion. But I think it is worth it to have a small discussion to find out what the purpose of religion is.

In my mind, the most important benefit anyone can get from religion is to understand the role of Gd in everyday living. I think that if there were no religion, it would be difficult for humanity to give value to things that are difficult to understand. Even if there were a great development in civilization and in the human mind, there still would be many questions that could not be answered, because the mind cannot give value to many things that are necessary for our everyday living.

A clear example of this is seeing great differences in the quality of the lives of people. Some are poor, some are rich, some are beautiful, and some are ugly. Some are smart and happy, and some are foolish and sad. The first thing that comes to mind is that the world is not fair. I do not think that the human mind can give easy reasons for these differences unless it believes that there is a Gd, and that there is a purpose behind all these differences. The collection of all these ideas, all these thoughts, and all this learning is called religion. The study and learning of religion tells us, and can convince us, to believe that the world is fair in spite of the seeming unfairness so we can continue to live in harmony. Is there another solution to these questions?

If it were not for religion, people could not have survived all the difficulties in the world throughout the centuries. Even with religion in the world, we can see that during the life of human civilization, many ideas and ideologies have come and gone. The purpose of all these ideologies was to answer the questions of the mind, but as you can see, none of those ideas has survived through human history.

I believe that piece of mind comes from religion, from the idea of Gd. For those who believe in a spiritual aspect of life, religion has even more meaning because it gives value to our actions. If not for Gd who sees everybody actions even after death, what would be the difference between a good and bad person if both of them had the same ending, the same death that everybody eventually will go through.

The next discussion about religion is the relation between science and religion. To many people, religious ideas cannot go along with science. To answer these people, we have to understand that religion is something completely different from science. Religion is an idea for the development of the human mind. There is no materialism in this at all. All religions in the world were created with enough flexibility to answer new scientific questions that have come and will come to humanity. Religion is for the human mind, and it will change with the human mind. Finding differences between science and religions is merely an excuse to blame religion for the misfortune of some people's lives. Simply put, religion is completely separate from science. I do not want to say that there is nothing scientific in religion, but religion has not come to improve science. Religion gives human civilization a special way of looking at the world. This guides us in how to live, what to expect, and what to follow.

The connection between religion and science is a very important one. In fact, science and religion should work together to build human civilization. That is the difference between our idea and the ideas of people like Bertrand Russell, who believed that knowledge and science were enough for the improvement and development of a proper civilization. I do not think anyone can deny the role of knowledge and science in improving life. The only thing I want to mention is that our lives are not just based on knowledge but also on faith. To me, religion and science should work together to build a society. There is no contradiction between the two at all. I believe that faith can have a significant role in our civilization, and that along with science; we can build a much better life for humanity.

Again, religions exist in the world, and our purpose is to find out if we should accept them or put them aside. If we put religions aside, that would be the end of the story, and there would be no way back to religions. We do not have the right to get away from religion completely, because we cannot be sure that one day in the future we will not find out that religion has an important role in our lives. In other words, even though we cannot prove religions at this time, we cannot set them aside unless we find out they are harmful to the world. Our purpose is to find a way to live without doubt, and we will be more confident with religions. I think religions are not against science but with science, and that they can build a better life for humanity.

At this point, I want to address two more questions that are important. First, what is real faith? When I talk about faith in this book, I am meaning a faith that can move a person, a true faith or belief that can change a life. Faith in Gd means that someone believes in Gd so much that, for him, nothing is more important than pleasing Gd, and everything else, including the best joys in this world, are not comparable to the happiness he gets from his faith in Gd. Such a person does nothing for himself. He does everything for Gd. This kind of faith is not the kind that can be found easily, but it should be the purpose of all human beings in the world. My goal in this book is to find true faith, which, in combination with true knowledge, can make a better life for all humanity.

This is the second question I would like to raise: is it possible to have faith in Gd without religion? I feel, this is not possible, because the purpose of faith in Gd is to know Him and to get close to Him. I mean if in our life we are supposed to get closer to Gd, this is not possible without help from Him, because He is the one that knows the way. We might be able to make a spiritual life by just having faith in Gd, but it is not going to be the kind of life that, in the end, brings us to knowing the creator. Knowing Gd means obeying his commands with spiritual and physical practices and requires a complete knowledge of his commands to humanity. The combination of all these things comes in an ideology that we call religion, and a true religion should come from Gd himself. Otherwise, we cannot say that religion can bring us closer to Gd.

As I mentioned before, my purpose in this book is not to prove religion; religions exist. I am only trying to understand our connections with the religions. Should we follow them? Should we obey their commands? Or should we put them away?

Now let me say another point. Maybe our minds cannot prove the concept of the religion at this time, but they cannot disprove it either. It means that even if we cannot find any benefit from religion in the whole history of humanity, we still cannot say for sure that religions are useless. The reason is that whatever we know about life and the world is from this time and some of the history from the past. We do not know the complete history from the past, and of course, we do not know the future. It is entirely possible that the whole purpose of religion is for the future of humanity. I am not talking about the next world. I am talking about this world. It means that there might be a moment in the future where religion can make a big difference in the life of a human being, and for that moment, Gd wants us to keep the religions alive. Again, religion came from Gd, and we have two choices: to either accept it or not accept it. If we want Gd, I think we have to accept religion also.

The next question comes to mind: What do we do if a religion is wrong? In other words, what if the commands in the religions are against our knowledge? I will discuss this important question in detail in the next chapter. I want to make this point again before we go on to the next chapter: as I said before, what we have to do is to find a way to get rid of doubt in our lives. We should find the best way possible to live with confidence. If we want to put away religion based on our knowledge at this time, there should be enough knowledge to uproot religion from its origins. It means that we cannot say that just because one command in a religion does not fit with our knowledge that we do not keep that religion anymore—we should know that our knowledge is limited. There can come a time when we find out that what we were thinking was wrong.

You can imagine that these kinds of religions need a lot of faith—faith in Gd, faith in goodness, and faith to find the goodness. It might be a difficult road to walk, but if there is no other, we should take this road. We should continue on this task until we find what we are looking for. Finding the truth in this world is not an easy task. Any person and any society who is not ready to take this road is going to be behind the others. This is the only road that our minds and hearts can take together.

The purpose of this chapter was to throw light on the life of those who believe in the truth and, with faith, take the load to find the right way of living. As I mentioned, this road leads to religion and Gd and hands up knowledge.

Reference:

1. *The Story of Civilization*, by Will Durant, volume 4, Page 175. Simon & Schuster, 1950.

Chapter 3
A TRUE RELIGION

In this chapter, we are going to answer a few more questions: which of the world's religions are acceptable? Should we accept all these religions? Which religions have stayed as they came from Gd? What should we do with false religions and false prophets? How can we identify false religions and false prophets?

As I said previously, if we could say that no religions had stayed the same as they came through Gd, it would be very easy to say that we do not have to obey any of them because we do not have the word of Gd.

Again, religion is an ideology that has come from Gd. He asks His followers to seek Him. By this definition, many religions cannot be considered a religion in this book. Buddhism is an example. Although it asks people to follow a good ideology, the basis of the ideology is not from Gd.

The other problem we encounter is that although we have few religions that we think came from Gd, each of these religions has been divided into branches. In other words, not all these branches can be true, and one, or maybe none of them, is the one Gd sent to us.

The other problem I mentioned is that of false prophets. A false prophet brings a false religion. What is the criteria distinguishing a true religion from a false one? We can rephrase the question another way: how can we find a true religion? A religion that came from Gd in the past, if it stayed the same, is a true religion, and if it changed, it cannot be called a true religion. If a prophet has brought a book from Gd, after we prove that the prophet was a true prophet, still we have to prove the book has not changed. Some religions, like Hinduism, do not know who their prophet was or who received the revelation to begin with.

If we look at religions, we will find out that many have accepted the fact that their original book might have been changed. The original book for religion is like the constitution for a country. If a country does not have a true constitution, the laws cannot be considered right. Some religions, like Zoroastrian religion, accept the fact that the original book from Gd has been lost (reference 1). They perform the orders from Gd, doing what they think Gd asked of them in the original book. Still, we do not have enough evidence now to believe that everything is the same as it originally came from Gd.

This problem exists in another way in Christianity. Whether Jesus was a prophet, or Messiah, or what have you has always been a question, but whether all four books in the New Testament are the original and complete books by Jesus is another question. Even the Church accepts that "sacred authors who wrote the four Gospels selecting some things from the many…" (reference 2). We can always argue that we follow a prophet, not a gospel, no matter how holy he was.

We have to pay attention to an important fact: a religion by itself is an order. By this, I mean that we have to obey the whole religion, and we do not have the power to distinguish which law and which command is right and which is not. In fact, this is the first order of religion. We have to accept it truly and obey all orders without exception. If we doubt one of the orders or laws of the religion and do not perform complete obedience, this not only contradicts our faith to one of the laws but also contradicts our faith to all of that religion. Simply, if we do not follow even one order of the religion because we think that order is wrong, we are automatically contradicting the whole religion. If a religion says that some of the orders or laws have been lost or have been changed from the original, each of us can say that what remains might have been changed or should have been changed too. In other words, how can we prove that what has been left for us is what Gd wanted for us from the beginning?

Now we can investigate a little further. If a religion has been divided into different branches, this division by itself means that some of the laws and orders have been changed through these divisions. In other words, each branch has laws and orders that are different from the others. Only if these laws and orders arise from different customs or different perceptions from religious authorities can they be accepted, provided that the basics are still the same. What I mean is that branching by itself is acceptable because of different customs and different environments that each of us has. But if these divisions and branching are so deep into the religion that the basics of it have been compromised, or the sources or authorities of the other branches have been questioned, this division suggests the loss of the original religion. If the differences are so basic, logically just one of the branches is right or all of them are wrong.

Now we are going to look at religions again. As we discussed, out of the major religions in the world, Islam is the only religion whose book, the Koran, has been accepted scientifically as the original book by the prophet. But Islam as a religion has major branches, and each of these branches has laws and orders, which are basically different from the other branches. Each of the branches has a source of laws and orders that are not accepted by the other branches. For example, if the authorities of one branch adopt a law, it does not have any acceptability by the followers of the other branches. By this, we can imagine that many of the laws that have come from Gd through the prophets may have been changed or lost. We can accept only those laws and orders as original if they have come through all the branches and they all have the same concept. Any laws and orders that do not go through all the channels have been lost through time. That is the reason Muslims have quotations that they call doubtful or mistaken words.

For example, a quotation from the prophets of the Muslims says, "Gd has created the Torah before he created the humankind" (reference 3). Now look at this quotation again. If it is right, it means that the Torah is a very important and valuable book. If a book has been created from the beginning of our creation, it should have important messages for humanity, and Gd had a purpose in bringing it to the world from the time of creation. We cannot easily say that this important book does not have any role in human life. But on the other hand, you can see that not all the authorities in Islam have accepted this quotation by the prophet, so which one is right? At the end, the Torah was created at the beginning of humankind or it was not?

So now what should we do? We can say that there is no religion we can trust 100 percent, and that we are not sure about words and laws in any religions that have come from Gd. We do not know what Gd wants from humanity. This is an important question and a complicated problem. Let's look at religions again.

First we will start with Judaism. The problem with Judaism is that there is no scientific evidence that Torah is the same book that was sent from Gd. Jewish clergy, of course, do not deal with this problem at all. They believe that the Torah is the same book that was sent to Moses and see no reason to discuss the issue at all. But as we said, if there is doubt, the doubt should be answered. If we do not answer the doubts in our minds, our functions will be wasted, and it will be difficult to find our goals in life.

In Islam, as we said, the Koran has some scientific basis, but the problem is the different branches in Islam and different quotations and laws in this religion. Some of these laws and quotations can be detrimental in our lives.

In Christianity and the Zoroastrian religion, some of the words from the prophets have been lost, and as we said, some of these words could have been important in our daily lives now. In other religions, like Hinduism, we do not know who the prophet was that Gd spoke to.

As you see, it can be hard to find the right track in this world. Even if you believe in Gd with all your heart, it is difficult to go toward him. Of course, we do not want religion to be daily prayer and daily service. We want something that gives us hope, gives us goals, and gives us the strength to be good. This is one of the hardest challenges in our lives right now. Are there any answers to our questions? I do not think anyone can say that he has the solution; it is our responsibility to find the truth, live with the truth, and stand for it.

I have some hints and tips that I think can help answer these questions. Of course, they are not the final answer, and the questions need much more research, investigation, and thinking, which demand that each one of us help push it forward.

Let's look at what we have so far. First, we said we believe in Gd. Second, we said there have been prophets that tried to make some communication between Gd and man. Third, out of all these prophecies, the only book we can scientifically say has been the same from the time of the prophets is the Koran. We think that if there is a Gd, there should be some sort of relationship between Him and us. This kind of relationship should be based on what Gd said to humanity. If Gd has created us and wants us to go toward Him, find Him, and join Him, He should have left us a kind of guidance in our life that we can hold and, with its help, move toward Him.

The question is if we can currently trust any of the religions in the world to have the complete word of Gd without any branching, changing, or doubt?

Let us look again at religions. What are the acceptable criteria for a religion to be a path to Gd? First, the religion should have come from Gd. How can we say that religion has come from Gd or not? There is no scientific way to answer this question because we do not know what Gd wanted from us, and we cannot go back to history and prove or disprove the religion by history. So the answer is that Gd has to tell us which of the religions has come from Him.

Again, belief in the Koran cannot be proved scientifically; this is just a belief. Even between the Muslims, there are questions about the Koran and the origin of the Koran, but almost for sure we can say it is the same book that was brought by the prophet. I think the Koran should be used as a base to know the religion. Without a base, we cannot prove or disprove any ideology in the world. The Koran mentions the names of the major religions: Judaism, Christianity, and other religions; some we know, and some we do not. It also states that a large number of prophets have received prophecy from Gd, but it does not say the names of the other religions. Based on the Koran, it would be hard to disprove the origin of some of the religions because the Koran does not bring the names of all the religions in the world.

After a book has come from Gd, the second criterion is that it should have kept the original words from Gd. Many people believe that a true religion should have the exact words of Gd. That means it should not have been changed through history, which sounds right. Of course, a true religion should have the words from Gd without any changes; otherwise, we cannot believe that what we are doing now is what Gd is asking us.

Of course, there are different opinions about the Koran, even among Muslims and Muslim authorities. But as I mentioned before, I think we can accept the book as being from Gd—that He wanted to give it to us and keep it safe through the generations to have a base for further delving into religion and faith. I think we should keep our faith, for the sake of finding out about religions. Gd and religion both are based on faith, and faith cannot be proved by science. The only purpose of this book is to show the compatibility between science and religion and living with true faith, which is based on logic and brings us closer to Gd in order to have a better life.

The only other book we can look upon is the Torah. Again, it has not been proved scientifically, but there is no reason to believe it has changed from its origin. If you look through the history and the origin of the Torah, you cannot find a good reason to believe it has changed; however, on the other hand, we cannot find a reason to believe that the book is the same book by Moses. Certainly, Jewish authorities and clergy believe in the Torah completely, with all their hearts. Belief in Torah is based mostly on faith rather than science. Anyone who needs to believe in the Torah has to study it completely, with all the different interpretations, and then he can say whether he believes in it. Personally, I do not see any reason to believe that the Torah has been changed through history.

Now let us see what the Koran says about the Torah. The Koran mentions in a few places that the Torah has a special problem. The Koran uses the word "Tahrif." Muslim authorities have different interpretations of this word. Some of them believe that the Torah has changed. Some believe that the interpretation of the Torah by the Jews was wrong, and some believe that the action of the Jews based on the Torah has been wrong. However, whatever this word means, we can always argue that the Koran could use a better word with a better meaning about the Torah. It could say that the Torah is not the original Torah, or it could say that the Torah is not usable anymore. On the contrary, the Koran never says this but does say that there is light and guidance in the Torah (reference 4). It is interesting that although there are differences between Islam and Judaism, and there are different quotations about the history, we cannot find any differences between the text of the Koran and the text of the Torah, when they write any particular story.

If you go through the Koran, you will not find any story that is different from the Torah. It might mention something more or something less, but there is no contradiction between the text of the Torah and the Koran, which I think is an important lesson for all people who believe in Gd and religions. I encourage those who cannot believe it to go through both the Koran and Torah and find a specific sentence or a specific story about anything in history that contradicts each other. Of course, I am not talking about the different laws in the Torah and the Koran, because the laws can be different for two different nations, but there are no specific differences in any historical text. I think you will agree that there is a great purpose behind all this.

I think there is a point that I have to reemphasize again, especially since we are talking about the Torah. We are trying to find the right way of living. It means that we have to search all the possibilities. We have to look upon all the facts and questions and find the best way out of them. About religion, and especially about Torah, I found it interesting that researchers took some of the questions as facts. If you look at the books that have been written about the origin of Torah, you see that the researchers have concluded that to them, the origin of the Torah is not clear.

They come with different questions, and after that, because they don't know the answers, they concluded that the Torah we have today is not the original. To me, this kind of conclusion is like living in the dark. If you are in the dark and cannot see anything, it does not mean that there is nothing there. If you come to the Jewish clergy and ask the questions, these questions are simple for them to answer. How can it be that something that is so simple to somebody can be so difficult for others to answer? If these groups of researchers have doubts about the Torah, it does not mean that everyone else believes the same idea they have. I think that if there is a doubt about something, it is our responsibility, instead of putting it away and forgetting about the question, to go and research the other possibilities.

We might not be able to use the Torah as the source for our discussion, but the nice thing about the Torah is that after the Koran, the Torah is the only book that its followers believe is the original book from God.

In short, I think we can accept the Torah as a book from Gd, and the reasons scientists think that the book has changed from its original are not strong enough to turn our faith away from it. It should be noted that what we are discussing here is all about faith—faith in Gd, faith in the Koran, and faith in the Torah. What we are doing in this discussion is bringing some logic to the faith. What we have discussed so far is that logic and science do not have enough proof to disqualify the three important issues in our lives: Gd, the Koran, and the Torah.

The discussion that remains is discussion about other religions. There are many other religions in the world, but we use the Koran to name the religions that Gd brought to humanity. It is also written in the Koran that there have been many more prophets from Gd to humanity, but their names are not found in the Koran.

As I have said, there are basic problems with other existing religions and books. We are not sure about the exact words of Gd. Even if even one word or one sentence has been changed, it can be very important and have many effects in our lives.

There is an important discussion about religion, which is as follows: if Gd has brought a religion to humanity and asked people to follow it, when the next religion comes along, does Gd ask the people to convert to the new religion? We will discuss this important question in detail in the next chapter. What I need to discuss at this point is what Gd wants from humanity? Gd has given us some laws, customs, and prayers, asking us to follow them. If his word, which was in the original book, is the law, do we have to follow the laws and the orders that He gave us?

If the original book has been changed or lost, there is no way that we can find his orders and his commands to humanity. This is the question that we can ask those religions that believe they have lost the original book or are not sure their original book is from Gd.

These questions are mostly for those religions that have lost their book, but even in Islam and Judaism, who believe they have the original book, these questions come to them. The point is, a religion is not just a book, although Islam and Judaism might have the original book, but there is no way that we can say the whole religion has stayed the same from the time of the prophets. It means that we do not have any clue if what we interpret from the book is the right interpretation Gd intended. It is never written in the Koran that the Torah has changed from its origins. What the Koran is saying is simply that the interpretation of the Torah might be wrong on a few or more points. Now we can imagine that humanity has two tasks: first, to find the original book; second, to find the right interpretation of the original book.

As we go through this book, I will discuss in more detail this problem and the solution that we currently have to the problem. I think I need to discuss one important point at this time. Human beings are not the owners of religion. That is, what we have in our hands as our religions is what Gd has given to us in the past. Gd gave us some rules and orders that we call religions. The first command of Gd was to obey Him and to follow His orders. We simply follow these orders to get closer to Gd. We have no idea for the reasons of many of these orders.

For example, if you look at the Torah or Koran, you can that see there are different orders that we do not have the reason for—certain types of foods that are permissible and other foods that are not permissible; certain things we can do and cannot do; different kinds of prayers we have to say and those that are not allowed. So why were all these orders and commands given to humanity? I think the reason is simple: Gd wanted us to know that by obeying and following his orders, we can get closer to him. We do all these things for Him, but the main purpose of a religion is not simply to keep these orders and traditions. I don't mean that order and laws in the religions are just given without any reason, but I feel that the main reason behind all these things might be something different.

There is no doubt that all these orders and laws are there to make a better person and a better community, but the way that Gd wanted to change humanity is not just simply to follow an order. Maybe what He really wanted from humanity is to learn how to follow Him and be in His way without any question and without searching for any reason. If we look at religion in this view, we can solve some of our problems about religions.

So how can we be sure that what we have right now is what Gd originally wanted from humanity? To answer this question, we should realize an extremely important point. If Gd ordered something to humanity and gave us rules and orders, but the reason behind the rules and orders was not completely clear to us, it would not be our responsibility to keep the religion in its original way because we didn't know the logic and philosophy behind all the orders. In the history of religions, there have been questions about many orders that people could not answer because they did not know the reasons behind them. It means that it can naturally be changed in different periods because of many different problems that humanity cannot easily solve. In other words, changing in religion is not always a human fault. I will clarify this point.

During history, humanity encountered many different problems, many different environments, and many different questions that we should have been able to answer, and we did. Answering any of these questions means finding a different way of living. If I want to make the question and answer a bit simpler, I should put it in a different way. Humanity is responsible for obeying Gd, obeying His commands only, but we have a limited capacity and cannot be responsible for what we cannot do. Keeping the religion in its original way is out of the power of humanity. We simply cannot be responsible for keeping the religion in its original form when Gd gave a religion to humanity; mistakes by human during history would be possible, and Gd knows it. So if humanity is not responsible for keeping the religion in its entire version, the way Gd ordered originally, who is responsible? I think the answer is Gd. Gd Himself has the responsibility to keep a religion alive and to keep it safe in a way that at any time in the life of humanity, anyone can have access to Gd. As human beings, we try to get closer to Gd and to His commands, and the rest is up to Him to accept it or not accept it.

Are all these religions that we follow real or just something that has simply been made by humans? A real religion is what Gd wanted from humanity, and He wants it at this very present time. On the other hand, whether what we are doing now is a true religion or not depends on how much we kept the original religion. If we do not know how much of our religion is true or not, the most we can do is use our pure minds and pure hearts to search for the true words of Gd.

Our resources are all the religions in this world. We have a few clues. We have the Koran, we have the Torah, and we have science and our minds. I think with a combination of all these resources, we have a good possibility of finding the right way because Gd has not closed the gate of truth and justice in the world. Maybe there is a reason that Gd did not want to show the way clearly to us. Maybe he wanted us to use our minds and hearts and all our other resources to find him.

Now we can go forward to ask a very hard question: How can we differentiate between a true and false religion? How can we say if a religion is true or not true? How can we say whether the laws in a religion are true orders from Gd or just some collection of what we have been gathering through the years and mixing with superstitions and other thoughts? In other words, how can we differentiate between a true religion from Gd and other false religions? Again, we have some criteria to accept a religion or not. First, the religion should not be against the Koran and the Torah, because they are the basis of our understanding from Gd. Second, the orders and laws in the religions should not be against science or logic. Third, which may be most important, is the faith and consciousness of humanity.

All three criteria have their own limitations. The Koran and Torah do not mention the names of all the religions. Names of many prophets are not known to us, so there have been many religions in the world that have been sent by Gd in the past but we do not know them About science and logic, you can imagine that science is changing all the time, and the human's logic changes throughout history, but I still believe that science and logic are one of the main keys of our understanding of the world. The third one is faith. Everything in religion starts and ends with faith. A true consciousness of human beings can certainly help. We cannot force anyone to accept any religion, and we cannot force anyone not to leave a religion. Everyone has freedom to go on the way he thinks is right. Perhaps this is the purpose of Gd: to leave humanity to choose the way he thinks is the right way, and in the end, Gd will judge us accordingly. As human beings, we have the responsibility to respect anyone's idea, as long as it is not against logic, science, Koran, and the Torah.

We will discuss in the next chapters about those religions that do not have a strong basis.

References:

1. *History of Zoroastrianism*, by Maneckji Nusservanji Dhalla, PhD, chapter 1. New York: Oxford University Press, London, Toronto, 1938.

2 Dogmatic Constitution on Divine Revelation, DEI VERBUM #19.

3 Sahih Bukhari, volume: 8, book: 77, Al-Qadar, #611. Also see Al-milal won Nihal by shahristani volume 1 for interpretation of the Hadith (quotation from the prophet).

4. Koran, Al-Maedeh; 44.

Chapter 4
CONVERSION

In chapter 1, we discussed that we believe in Gd. In chapter 2, we mentioned that there is evidence that a kind of relationship and communication between humanity and Gd has existed in the past. In chapter 3, we proved that these relationships and religions are still alive and we can follow them to get closer to Gd. In this chapter, we will discuss in detail about the roll of conversion. Are people obliged to convert from an old religion to a new religion? The other question is what we should do with an old but practicing and loved religion. Is there any use of the old religions?

We said, religion is the relationship between Gd and humanity. Gd has written a religion like a constitution and sent it to humanity. He left us free to obey this constitution. There has been no judge and no observer through history that humanity is really keeping the laws as they were ordered originally. Gd left us alone in this matter. He let us do what we thought was right. We could obey religion, we could disobey religion, and we could do anything to change the religion as we wanted it. Gd sent a religion to us, and after that, we don't know what our ancestors have done to the religion. Gd almost never punished any nation for changing the religion. In other words, Gd gave us religion and said that it is ours, we can do what we want to do with it. I think that behind this concept, there is one very important point.

If we are alone with what we have it means that this is all ours. The religion that Gd gave us is just for us. What we gain from it is for us, and what we don't gain from it is our loss. A simple result of this matter is that the religion Gd has given us, became a part of our life. Belief in religion and the laws that Gd gave us, both serving a bigger concept, our daily life. If these laws have been changed through history, it has affected our lives substantially. Through the history of humanity, religion and the lives of religious people have been so connected that it is difficult to separate them from each other.

Essentially, if a religion has been changed through history, it does not mean that the religion has been lost. The religion is still alive as long as its followers are alive. Religion and humanity are so much attached, which, sometimes is hard to say whether this is a religion or the custom of the people who are observing it. A religion is still alive as long as it has some followers. When Gd gave us the command to obey religion, there was no condition in it. The followers still have the command from Gd to obey the religion. If a religion has now changed, it is up to Gd to decide whether what the followers are doing is what He wants. Nobody else in this world has the authority to tell people that what they are doing is right or wrong. The only words we have from Gd are in the Koran and the Torah. If the Koran or the Torah has rejected a religion, it means that that religion is not valid anymore by Gd. But if the Koran or Torah does not mention anything about a religion, no one else has the authority in this world to disprove the religion.

Now I am going to discuss conversion. I need to state at this point that accepting other religions by itself does not mean conversion. If a Jew believed that Koran had been sent from Gd, he has not changed his religion to something else. Faith has different branches and different objects. We can have faith in the truth and follow the truth, but conversion means changing the lifestyle and the way of living. I need to repeat this question: Are we obliged to change our lifestyles to new ones after accepting other religions? For example, if a Jew accepts the Koran that has been sent from Gd, is he obliged to change his religion?

I am going to discuss this subject in two different formats: first, a discussion about conversion now, and then conversion at the time of the prophets. I need to point out here that what we are discussing is truly based on logic. Logic is different from faith. Religions are not based on logic alone. Religion is a mixture of faith and logic. Many times in religion, faith overcomes logic. In short, what we are discussing logically does not necessarily mean that everybody will faithfully follow it. But in our society, we judge people based on logic. The laws and orders in our societies are based on logic, and I believe that Gd also judges people based on logic, and He would not punish any person if he wanted to do something based on logic. Again, I do not expect all religious people in the world to accept what I am discussing here, but on the other hand, I hope people can realize a pure and genuine logic.

What I hope to convey in this chapter is that I do not think conversion is currently an order, and that everyone has the freedom to search, think, and choose. My reasons for this:

1. The first reason is what we discussed in chapter 3. When we talk about conversion, we are talking about conversion from one religion to another. The problem with the new religion is branching. As mentioned, Islam, Christianity, and many other religions have different branches, and these branches have basic differences. If it was just one new religion that we knew for sure had the word of Gd

and all the laws and orders from Gd had been kept clean and clear, then the problem of conversion would be solved because it was the responsibility of everyone to go and hear the word of Gd. Currently, although we believe that the Koran has the word of Gd, the religion of Islam is not just limited to the Koran, and of course, conversion is not just about believing in the Koran. Conversion means changing the whole lifestyle to a new one. In the next few chapters, we will discuss in more detail the purpose of all these differences? Why we cannot be 100 percent sure about any religion, and why Gd didn't make the religions in a way that we can say for sure is the right way to go.

2. The second reason is that conversion does not fit with the training. What I mean by that is that if a religion would say that you might have to change your religion in the future, this would, by itself, be contradicting the religion. If a religion cannot stay forever and has to change at some point to a new religion, none of the followers can believe fully in that religion. How can someone train his children and his students and ask them to put everything in their life for this religion, but you should know that in the future you might have to convert to another religion. Why should someone try to learn all his life the laws and orders that may change at some point in the future? As you see, all the religions are saying that what they are teaching is forever and will not be changing in the future. This is a fundamental thing for training.

I can give you an example. Imagine that your child is learning a hard foreign language in school, and he puts all his effort into learning what the teacher is teaching. Now, at some point, someone comes and tells you that the plan has changed, and that your child does not need that language anymore. How would the child feel then? Would you be willing to have your child learn any other language?

3. Reason number three is a problem of confidence. The problem is that conversion needs faith and confidence. If someone wants to change his religion and convert to a new one, he has to change a big portion of his lifestyle. He might have to change many of his friends; he might not be able to talk to many of his family members anymore; and he should be ready to have a difficult time for at least a period of his life. Now the question is, is he obliged to do such a thing or not? Is there another solution to this problem? Does Gd want him to do such a thing or not? We need 100 percent confidence in all these questions. If there is even a 1 percent chance that Gd wants him to stay in his religion, I am sure that almost all of us would take that chance.

Conversion is a difficult task, and we cannot ask anyone to convert unless we can assure him 100 percent that what he is doing is what Gd wants him to do. We will discuss a little bit more in detail, if we have enough reason to believe, this is what Gd wants us to do or not.

4. The next problem with conversion is convincing the people that their religion is not good anymore. For example, take the Jews and tell them that Torah is no good anymore. The first question that they will ask is why. The Jews don't think the Torah has changed and see no reason that what they have been doing is not enough. If the Torah came from Gd, as they believe, and there have been no changes in the Torah, what would be the reason that they would have to change their religion to the new religion of Christianity. In addition, those that have read the Torah and the culture of Judaism know how big the culture is. I can say for sure that it is practically impossible to convince an orthodox Jew that what he has been doing so far is no longer adequate, and that the new religion has better laws and orders. If anyone has doubts about it, he should go and learn the Torah for himself; he will find out how hard it is to say that a new religion has come from Gd and you have to forget all about the Torah. In other words, the older religions do not believe that they need a new religion. As discussed, we cannot say for sure that the Torah changed and is not the original anymore. If we cannot prove that the Torah is not the original, then we have to explain many other things. If we believe that the Torah is the same Torah that Gd has sent to humanity, then how can we say that the Torah should not be learned anymore or discussed anymore, that all the learning from the Torah should be forgotten?

This is the reason that Muslims claim that the Torah is not the original Torah, because otherwise how can they say Jews have to forget the Torah and convert to the new religion? Even between Judaism and Christianity, this problem arises again. Although Christianity believes in the Torah and the Old Testament, Christian authority always tries to say that Jesus has ended the learning of the Torah, and that Jesus changed all the laws and orders of the Torah. The problem with this kind of teaching by Islam and Christianity is that they have to have a good reason for why the religion changed. What new thing did they bring to the world? If a Jew has to change his religion, he has to know why Gd is asking him to forget all he learned from the Torah and start a new religion all over again. What is a Jew missing from learning the Torah that he will gain from learning the Koran?

In summary, if groups of people have the word of Gd, they have the right to keep those words, and the only authority that can tell them and ask them to change their religions is another word from Gd. Otherwise, no one else has that authority to ask the people to forget what they have gotten from Gd. We will discuss in detail about the conversion at the time of a prophet.

5. The next problem has more to do with the rights of an individual. Conversion is an extremely difficult undertaking. For example, for an elderly person who has spent all his life with a religion he believed was right, it would be difficult to change his religion, which automatically is going to change his lifestyle. The question is whether Gd asked for such a difficult action. Not everyone is like Abraham. We should emphasize one point here—that conversion is not because a religion is wrong or the followers were doing something that was wrong. If that was the reason, Gd could simply bring another prophet to tell them the right thing to do. But if Gd brings a new religion that is completely different from the previous one, it means that the reason behind conversion should not be that what they were doing was wrong. The reason that people have to convert would be that a new religion has come to the world, and this is difficult for many people to understand. The basic question is, why should Gd do such a thing? Why would he bring a different religion with different ideas and each time ask the people to change their religion to the new one? Understanding these concepts is difficult, and the questions are hard to answer. I doubt that Gd would ask such a difficult thing from humanity.

6. This final point I am going to make is a practical one, and it goes back to the first reason. The question is, even if someone wants to convert and has to convert, which branches of the new religion does he choose after he decides to change his religion to the new one? Again, there are many branches in the new religions, in Islam, Christianity, and other religions, so which one of these branches does the person choose? We should note that choosing between the branches is harder than choosing a religion. A religion has a book and a prophet, and you can simply go to the book and see what a religion is saying. And if you think this book has come from Gd, you can convert if you want, but how can you decide which branch is right and which one is wrong? Choosing between the branches, you would have to be a scientist and historian to know the answer. As we said, sometimes differences between the branches are as big as the differences between religions. What would be solved with the conversion? There would still be one religion with different branches, and everything would be the same as now. We go back to the same problem.

What I've discussed so far was the problem of conversion now, and to me, conversion is not the solution for the differences of religions in the world. In the next chapters, I will discuss the solution for the unity of the religions, but at the end of the chapter, I still have to discuss the problem of conversion at the time of the prophets.

When a prophet comes and brings a new religion, the question is different. The question is not whether the religion is right or not because we have the prophet, who has a connection to Gd. So we can go to him and ask him all the questions. If the prophet says someone has to change his religion, there is no reason for someone not to do so. But I don't believe that any prophet has said that the followers of the old religion have to change to the new one. They brought a new religion to the world and asked the people to listen to the word of Gd, but I don't believe that Gd would ask the people to change their religion and forget what he told them in the past. I believe that everyone has to believe and accept the word of Gd, but the conversion is something much above the acceptance of the word of Gd. I don't think this was an order from Gd.

I don't find any discussion in the Koran that followers of other religions have to change and convert. What the Koran always asks is to accept the Koran as the word of Gd, but the obligation to convert and throw away your previous religion is not understood from the Koran (reference 1). In the Koran, even Moses and Aaron are called Muslims (reference 2). I encourage everyone to read the Koran, although the interpretation of it is on the shoulders of the authorities but they should also accept the problems with the conversion.

I believe that the same applies to the conflict of Christianity and Judaism. Although there is no proof for this, my understanding from early Christianity is that Jews were supposed to accept Jesus but not to forget their religion. Again, it is up to the Christian authorities to assess this concept.

I will discuss later the other possibilities that might have been in Gd's mind when He sent a new religion to the world, conversion was not the only solution.

References:

1. Koran, Aal-Omran; 199; "There are groups from previous religions who believe in your book and their book… Those groups will have good rewards…"

2. Koran; Al-Aaraf; 126

Chapter 5
A MIXTURE OF RELIGIONS

As we discussed, we believe in Gd and need some kind of relationship with Him, so we believe that he has sent prophets to us to establish this relationship. Again, humanity has an obligation to obey religion because it is an order from Gd. The whole purpose of keeping religion is having a relationship with Gd. Any order in a religion should be obeyed unless the order is against logic or if it will destroy a life. In such a case, we can guess that the order has not come from Gd or has been changed through history. Otherwise, any order in a religion should be obeyed completely, without a second thought.

We then mentioned that conversion from one religion to another does not have a logical base, but besides this, we believe that none of the religions has said that a person has to convert. Any religion that came later always respected the previous religion; this respect is an order from Gd, although many may feel otherwise. In other words, if a person believes in Gd completely, no one in the world can tell him what religion he has to obey. It is only between him and Gd to decide which religion he will keep in his life. No one in this world can say who is closer to Gd.

If we imagine that people can obey different religions, how is it possible to make a kind of communal relationship among religions? Are the religions contradicting each other? How is it possible that Gd gives different orders at different times? How can a Christian or Muslim respect another religion whose orders are completely different from his or her own? How is it possible for all these different laws to be right and suitable for humanity? Why did Gd make all these differences between the religions?

At this point, I want to discuss a basic question before moving on to the others. What is the relationship between religion and science? Is religion enough without science? The answer is no. Everyone knows we need science. What about the sciences of psychology and sociology? Can religion replace these sciences for us? I think the answer again is no. Now the question is, if humanity needs psychology, sociology, and medicine, etc., what is the role of religion? Why do we need it? The answer is that religion was not given to teach us science.

Science is a burden on us because we have to go out and discover it. But religion is something else that humanity cannot build on its own. This is what I have said in the previous chapters. Religion is a relationship that we need with Gd to give us a sense of security in this life and even after death. He needs religion to give him a sense of bravery, kindness, goodness, and happiness. Again, we do not create religion; religion is here, and all we can do is take it or leave it. On this basis, we can now begin to understand why religious people think this is the best way of living. On the other hand, we can understand how science is important in human life—because religion cannot replace the sciences at all. We believe that there should not be any contradiction between science and religion. Any laws that are against science are wrong, unless the scientific finding was not correct.

Religion is essentially telling us to go learn how to live. Discover this world. Find the finest sciences and then you will know you need Gd. On the other hand, science cannot differentiate between religions unless one of the religions completely contradicts sciences, of which I do not know any. So, if sciences cannot differentiate between religions, it means that the human mind may never be able to differentiate between religions, to accept one and set aside another. I do not mean that humanity is not able to find false religions, and that there is no way we can recognize a true religion. All I mean is that if a religion has come from Gd, humanity does not have the power to deny or refuse that religion at any time. If something has come from Gd, the only one who can change or completely erase the words is Gd himself.

If this is the case, what should humanity do with all the different religions of the world? If someone wants to keep a religion from the beginning, how can he find the best one? To answer this question, let us examine the basic laws and orders of the religions. I believe that Gd has given us different religions for a purpose only he knows. We will discuss a few theories about why different religions have come to the world. At this point, I want to emphasize one thing: even though he has brought different religions to the world, all these orders have come from Him. All the religions of the world obey the orders that have the same spectrum. What I mean by that is that even though Islam and Judaism have completely different orders, if you look at them closely, you can see that all the orders can be categorized in the same classes.

For example, both believe that one day a week should be taken off from work, although the laws of Sabbath are completely different from the orders Islam gives for Friday, but we can see that the spirit of having a day off is there. This is true about all other orders—for example, about eating different foods, about fasting, about prayers, and all kinds of different laws in the religions. Of course, there are many differences between them, but because both have come from Gd, they follow the same path to Gd, and that is probably what Gd wants to achieve. He wants to establish paths from us to Him, and we have the power to choose between those paths.

The problem religion faces is that people cannot accept that Gd can bring different orders and different religions to the world. We as humans cannot determine what Gd wants to do. The only question we can ask is whether it is possible that all religions will achieve the same goal in the end. All I can say is that at least we don't have enough reason to believe that this cannot be true. We do not have enough reasons to say that there is only one way, which is accepted by Gd, and no other way. Even in our society, if we look carefully, we can see that there are different laws for different people. I am not talking about rights—everyone has the same rights—but the orders one has to follow in his life, which depend on how he was brought up, how he wants to live, and where he is living. Because of different backgrounds, societies, and cultures, a person living in America does not necessarily have the same laws or orders as a person living in Japan, South Africa, or Iran. Look at medicine, psychiatry, or sociology. A doctor does not prescribe the same prescription for everyone. Not everyone needs to avoid fat or meat. Not everyone has to avoid certain drugs or foods. Even in the same religions, different groups in the religion can have different orders. A man and woman do not necessarily have the same orders. We cannot rule out the possibility that what Gd wanted from the beginning was to have different religions that all achieve the same goal; maybe what he wants from us is to keep on the paths and go toward him in peace and harmony.

The other problem is that most people believe that one religion is best for humanity. This is especially true about religions that came later in human history. Later religions are essentially saying that the time for the former religions has ended, and it is time to change to something new. I do not know how or where this thought came from, but I can say that we do not have any word from Gd that one of the religions He sent us is better than the other. If we look at the Koran, we can find many places where He asks humanity to live in peace and harmony, to respect each other, and to follow his commands, which have come through the prophets.

If we think about this as a social problem, we can easily see that it is not possible to define which religion is better or complete. How can we say that Gd has sent religions to the world, which, were not complete and we should not follow them at present time. Isn't it confusing? To me, this is not only confusing but illogical as well.

I need to mention that through human history and the history of religions, all the religions have called themselves the best and most righteous. Otherwise, none could keep its followers. But even if we suppose that one of the religions is best, it does not mean that the others are not good. There is no way we can determine which is best.

In summary of this discussion, humanity is following what Gd has given us. He has brought a few religions to the world. For us, it is not possible to determine which is best. Also, we do not have any reason to believe that just one path and one religion is the right one. This is what we see in our current society. Now the question is why the religions cannot accept each other and live together in peace and harmony. The answer is not so difficult to find. The problem is that each of the religions calls itself the best. This is probably the key to keeping their followers. If they do not show themselves as being the most complete religion, ultimately their followers will not be convinced.

Don't get me wrong. I am not saying that all religions are the same; maybe one of them is the best. I do not want to interfere with any ideology or belief that anyone might have. It is possible that one could be better than the other is.

What I am saying here is that even if one is better than the other is, there is no proof that the others are not good enough and that Gd would not accept the followers of another religion. We can all decide for ourselves which path to follow. It is up to Gd to look at our hearts and minds and decide who will be accepted. Each religion can call itself the best, but it does not mean that its follower should not tolerate the others and fight with them. If a religion makes the best followers, they can prove themselves by their actions. Our actions are the only proof of our religion; otherwise, we cannot decide among them at all, and it will be up to Gd to decide.

I again advise anyone who thinks he can decide and choose the right religions to go and study them in full depth. This means to go to their schools and study them in their own languages, live with them as they live, and then decide if he can choose between them. I refer you again to what Al-Biruni said in his book a few centuries ago (reference 1).

The main purpose of religions is to give faith to humanity. Faith is the only way to shape a person and keep a person moving on a path toward Gd. The problem with faith is finding the right one. So how can we find a true religion?

If any religion changes the word of Gd, that religion is no longer accepted. It would be a great challenge to find the true religions, but I am going to give a few clues in the next chapter. For the sake of this discussion, I have to say that it is possible to find a true religion and to keep peace and harmony between religions.

The other question that needs an answer is about possibility of contradiction between our theory and the principles of religions. If the clergy and religious authorities vote against our theory and think what is being discussed here is against their religions, then what should be done? The theory we are presenting now should be in concordance with all the religions. That is, we cannot say anything that is against the principles of the religions, and we should not say anything that contradicts them. Therefore, if the religions' authorities do not accept our theory, we are not going to have any more discussion. We are presenting this theory to them. No one has the power to find a new way for himself. We all move together. We just bring the questions and try to answer them according to the principles of the religions. I want to emphasize the point that no one has the right to create a new religion, combine any, or change them in any way. Each individual can have faith or belief and can live his own way of living, but as a group and a society, we cannot make new religions for ourselves.

As I mentioned in the first chapter, religion is what Gd has given to us. The only reason we go after a religion is that it exists now, we do not intend to find a new religion or to mix the religions together. The first way that we should resolve diversity is by avoiding further diversion. We cannot go against religions' authorities, because without them, any religion can go in the wrong direction.

I do not intend to say that religions have been right all the time throughout history. If we want to find the right way and correct the mistakes that religion have encountered through history, we must avoid what has been done wrongfully in the past. We have to find peace and harmony between religions as they are right now, and it is the duty of each of us to study religions in depth and to find the right way to find this harmony. As a guide, this book may be helpful for this purpose. I believe that what I have written in this book is compatible with the Koran and Torah, but if any of the authorities believe this theory is not compatible with their religion's principles, I have no right to push this idea to them. I leave to the authorities of religions the discussions of whether this book and this theory are on the right track. I do not have the authority to go into detail about any religions, but I hope the authorities will not find anything against their principles in this book.

Now we will move on to a more basic question. What is the reason for that many religions in the world? Why has Gd created so many? Wasn't it better for Gd to create just one religion, keeping it throughout history and trying to convince people to keep it? I feel this fundamental question rises in the minds of everyone. There is so much fighting between the different religions. Almost every day you hear the news about all these mini wars between religions all around the world. This is a common statement you hear from nonreligious people: "Because there is so much fighting between religions, I think they are all wrong and see no reason to follow any of them." If you believe in one of these religions, usually the authorities give you a reason for all the differences. For example, in Islam, there is a theory that other religions came to make people ready for Islam. In Christianity, they believe that when Jesus came, he had the power to make things easier and make the religions much simpler. In Judaism, the belief is that the main religion is Judaism and the other religions are not as deep and sophisticated as it is.

If someone studies all these religions in depth, he can understand the reason behind all these different theories. It is not so hard for the followers of the different religions to accept these theories. I do not intend to discuss any of these theories. They might be right or they might not be, but not all of them can be right at the same time. What we are experiencing is intolerance between religions. Maybe that is the reason all these religions are waiting for someone to come from Gd and prove his position. Until that time, no one can prove or disprove any of these theories.

As mentioned in previous chapters, even if we accept any of these theories, there are still many questions that need to be answered. For example, how can we know if one religion is better than another? How do we solve the problem of conversion? How can we solve the problem of branching in religion? How can we unite the many good people in different religions who have dedicated their lives to Gd, and their lives are the symbols of true faith? We can see these good people who have gone on different paths through different religions, but they all have the most effective tools to unite, a beautiful faith on Gd and a selfless devotion to truth.

All these theories are just explanations for what is going on in the world. We might not even find the true reason Gd had in mind for all the different religions. Whatever we say might not be right or might not be the only reason for this purpose. I do not think we can prove any religion as the best religion, and I do not think it would be possible to have had just one religion—and we could have kept this religion, without any mistake or further branching—through history. Human beings have the power of thinking. They can choose and do what they think is right. Gd created man to think and grow. Now, without power, look at what we have done to religion. Even between the followers of a religion, not everyone keeps the same spirit of the religion as there was at the time of the prophets. They have all been branching to different sects. Sometimes we can see that the differences between the branches are much more deeper than the differences between religions. We see fighting and war between the branches of one religion, and we certainly see no unity even among the people of one religion. So, if it is going to happen to one religion, why shouldn't Gd have brought a few more religions to the world? If we cannot be united in one religion, why can't we have a few more religions? Do we think that if there were only one religion, there would be less fighting? I do not think so.

We should note that differences between the branches are much more difficult to solve than differences between the religions because among the branches, we can say for sure that one is wrong, and many times the differences are very deep into the roots of the religions. One of the differences between religions and branches is that we know for sure that humans created branches, but the religions themselves were created by Gd. If you want to make a union between the branches of one religion, they would have to forget their differences and follow the same path. They should forget the branching and try to unite from the beginning. In other words, you have to correct what humans have done and do it right from the beginning. Between the religions, this is not the case. Gd has brought them to humanity. We do not have the right to prove or disprove anything that has come from Gd. It is the responsibility of Gd to show that one is right and one is not. We will discuss this subject in the next chapters, but right now, I need to emphasize again that the religions we are discussing here have all come from Gd. We as humans do not have the power to say which is right or not. Even if one of the religions is better than another is, as long as we follow any path that Gd has brought in the past, we are still on the path to Gd. That is the fundamental principle.

I need to point out that if Gd had created just one religion, we wouldn't have been united around one religion; we would have been divided into different branches that are much more difficult to unite. In fact, I think that the only reason people in different branches of one religion are tolerating each other is that there are different religions around them, and the other religions make them feel they have to unite within their own. If there were only one religion, the differences between the branches of that religion would be much deeper than they now are.

What I want to conclude from this discussion is that even if we do not know the reason behind all the different religions, we can say one thing for sure: it is our responsibility to find the right way of living and to find peace and union. Gd has helped humanity grow by bringing religions to the world. This is the famous philosophy that through the differences, we can find union. We are going to discuss this matter in the next chapters, but I want to mention briefly that different religions are to make peace and unions between humans and help us to grow. Instead of looking at the differences, it may be better to look at the similarities. The religions are all fundamentally similar, and any person who follows a religion in the right way is accepted by Gd and should be accepted by humanity. Different religions should give us more faith because we can see that all have the same fundamental principles. Maybe that's all what we have to do : to look at the religions with an open eye without all the prejudgments, then the other differences can be easily solved.

At the end of this chapter, I want to answer one more question that may have arisen at this time. If someone is not following any religions and wants to be religious, which one should he choose? Can we tell him he should go and pick this one or another? I want to say at this point that it is quite possible that one is better than another. As human beings, we have the right to choose. Everyone has to research for himself and find which one is best for him. In the end, each person is responsible for his or her actions. All of us can have faith in our religions. We can say that ours is best. There is no problem with this, and maybe actually this is a true faith. The only thing that is not right, and which we have to avoid, is rejecting other religions and other ideas. Any idea that has come from Gd should be accepted by society and by our minds. Although we should observe the religions thoroughly and not change any laws, we should still be aware that there might be other paths to Gd, and Gd might accept these other paths. He will be the ultimate judge in the future. Let Gd be the judge.

We have a responsibility to find the best way for ourselves; we do what we can do and what is in our hearts. We should find true faith, and we should make the best of this world. Religions are not a simple thing. They need lots of research and faith. The problem did not start now and will not be solved now. It is the challenge of humanity to find the best way of living, and this challenge is going to continue for all time. All we can do is to make this challenge easier by tolerating other ideas about religion and by researching with a pure heart.

Reference:

1. Athar-ul-Bakiya, The Chronology of Ancient Nations, by Al-Biruni, translated by C. Edward Sachau, William H. Allen and Co. London, 1879. I briefly quoted some of it in the preface.

Chapter 6
TRUE FAITH

We started this book with the idea that we believe in Gd—and if there is a Gd, there should be a relationship between Him and humanity, and we call that relationship a religion. Then we discussed the idea that there should be at least one written contract between humanity and Gd, and that written contract most probably is the Koran. We also discussed the idea that this contract is not the whole relationship. A religion is more than a book. We then made the point that if other religions in the world accept Gd and the right concept of Gd, and if He sent them to humanity, they are still alive. There is no reason to believe that the followers of other religions have to convert to a new religion. What is important is to have a right and true concept of Gd and religion, which, which can help humanity to make a peaceful and happy world.

In the last two chapters, we looked at this concept and tried to answer many questions that can potentially be brought up. The material in this chapter is going to be more difficult to discuss because it is going into more detail, though I will try to avoid delving too deeply into the details of the questions because they are still not completely clear to anyone. As I stated previously, the whole theory should be discussed more in the future, and all we are discussing here is an opening for a new idea.

One of the main questions that you hear mostly in Western countries is how we can believe that Gd has sent any religion to humanity. As we discussed, if we believe in Gd, we should believe that there is at least one religion in the world that is alive and maintaining a relationship between humanity and Gd. If we go into a bit more detail, I can conceive that all we need are the words from Gd. By that, I mean that we should have at least one complete document from Gd that contains the words of Gd. This document is not necessarily a religion but a book that we believe has maintained the words of Gd.

In the Eastern world, where there is more of a belief in religion, the questions are different. They do not usually have questions about the origins of religion, because in the Eastern world, there is usually a belief in Gd and the belief that there have been religions in the past. The question is whether the books Gd sent to humanity are maintained in the right way.

I am not going to discuss Western philosophy that much. I believe the problem originates from the basic question of whether or not Gd exists. Again, the belief in the existence of Gd is hard to prove, and in this book, we are not trying to explain the reasons for the existence of Gd. I just want to mention one point: belief in Gd means belief in our ability to answer his questions. Without Gd, I do not believe we are able to answer our main questions about this world, coming into it or leaving it. Without Gd, there is no reason to believe that there is a life after this.

Eastern philosophers, although they mostly believe in Gd and in religions, surprisingly are still using Western philosophers to prove their own ideas. If you think about it, it is easier to understand the Eastern philosopher, but it is sometimes surprising to me how a philosopher who believes in Gd can disprove the relationship we have with Gd. What I mean by that is that a Jewish or Christian philosopher, if he truly believes in Gd, should understand that each one of us needs a kind of relationship with Gd. If the Torah, for example, has been lost, how can a Jew claim that he has any connections or a link to his Gd?

In Eastern countries, the problem is somehow different. Most people and almost all the philosophers have some kind of belief in Gd and some kind of belief in a book. For example, Muslim philosophers believe in the Koran, and Jewish philosophers believe in the Torah, but as we discussed, they do not believe in each other. In addition to this, there have been many branches in some of the religions, and each branch believes in different laws that sometimes are completely different from the other branches. All these things have made a kind of chaos in Eastern countries, and as a result, you see war. But still I can say that I understand these differences between the religions much better than Western philosophy, in that they believe in Gd without belief in any book or religions. To me, most of this reasoning is not genuine and pure but is originating from our desires, as I discussed in the preface of this book.

Now we will try to analyze the differences in Eastern philosophy among religions. I do not have the authority to go to each religion and find out which law is right and which is not. I am simply mentioning some basic facts that all the religions have been based on. We can therefore reach a conclusion that all religions and all branches can accept.

To start this discussion, I will begin with the Torah, as I think it can serve as one of the best clues to solve this problem. As I said in previous chapters, besides the

Koran, the Torah is the only book whose followers believe it is the same book sent from Gd. As far as the other books—even the New Testament, for example—although the Christian authorities believe in them, no one claims that they are the exact word from Gd to the prophet. This is a basic point because we base our lives on the word of Gd, from Him to the main prophet of the religion. This is the only way that we can discuss any religion. For a religion to be accepted by people, it should have the word of Gd to the prophets, without any changes during the whole of human history. As I mentioned, there are only two books in the world, the Koran and the Torah, that their followers believe are the words of Gd. We discussed the Koran in previous chapters, stating that it is the basis of our theory and belief. Again, about the Torah, there is not enough proof to believe that it is not the same book that Gd sent to Moses. Now I will discuss the importance of the Torah.

I think the Torah is the clue to the solution of our problems. Almost all religions besides Judaism and Islam have accepted the fact that the word of Gd them is not completely found in their religion. It means that the authorities of these religions believe that although they have the spirit of Gd in their religions, there is no more exact word of Gd kept throughout history.

As we discussed before, although these religions are still accepted, if the words of Gd are lost, there would be one problem. If Gd has asked them to convert to a new religion later on and now the word of Gd is lost, we don't know if these religions can be accepted anymore. In other words, if a religion has lost the word of Gd, it cannot be accepted as a religion, because we don't know that what has been kept in the religion is what Gd has been asking them. To prove the point that these religions are still accepted by Gd, we should have proof that Gd wants them to follow the religion as their fathers have been following. To make this point short and simple, I should say, for the sake of the theory, that at least one more book besides the Koran should have been kept completely and without any changes, and that is the key to our problem. The key is the Torah.

If someone believes that the Koran is the only book that has been kept without change in the history, then he is obligated just to follow this book and this religion. If there are two books that have remained clean and complete through the history, then one can challenge one book with the other and one religion with the other. Once two religions have been accepted, we can then automatically assume that even more than two religions can exist in the world. Let me make this point a little clearer. If we accept the Koran as the only book that has the exact word of Gd and there is no other book, then everyone in the world has the obligation to convert to Islam because it would be the only religion that has the word of Gd. Before I go further, I should make the point clear again about the word of Gd; this means the exact words that Gd gave to the prophet; this would be the base and constitution of the religion. If a religion does not have the exact words of Gd to the prophet, the religion is without a constitution. Other books in the religion, although the writer may have had the holy spirit from Gd, are still not as holy as the word from Gd Himself; that is more holy that any other thing.

Someone might ask what the problem would be if everyone converted to just one religion. We discussed this in previous chapters, but briefly, converting everyone to one religion potentially has a few problems. The main problem is that Islam by itself is not just one religion. It has been changed to many branches through history, and now each of the branches of Islam has different orders. After converting everyone to just one religion, we are not going to have one religion for everyone, we are going to have many branches of Islam in the world, and we can imagine that potentially we would have the same problem we have right now. For more discussion about this point, I refer you to previous chapters.

Going back to the Torah, I need to emphasize the point that by accepting the Torah and the Koran together, we can imagine that Gd can accept more than one religion. If two religions are acceptable then it is possible that other religions are also more or less acceptable. Although each religion has different levels, one cannot call the other religion a dead one. We believe that the Koran and the Torah are two books that have clearly been sent from Gd and have His word. Other books and prophets may have the word, but no other religions currently claim that they have the exact word of Gd. Anyone who believes in the Koran or Torah should have the basic faith that the word of Gd has not changed. If someone does not believe in this basic fact, then his belief cannot be complete and right. These two books can serve humanity together and help find the best solutions for life. These two books can make common ground for all religions in the world, causing unity between them.

Now let us discuss the Torah in a little more detail. Those who do not believe in the Torah are likely from one of two different origins: the Western philosophers and the Muslim philosophers. Let's start with the Muslims.

They generally believe that the Torah has been changed from its origin. It is interesting that the Koran never mentions this, and there is even admiration for the Torah in the Koran. But the Koran has stated that the Jews have done something to the Torah. What the Koran used for this action of the Jews is a word with many different interpretations. The word that Koran used is "Tahrif." It is interesting that even the Muslim authorities believe that this word has many different meanings. As discussed previously, some of the interpreters of the Koran believe that even Koran also has gone through Tahrif (but the majority disagrees with them.)

Those people with a background in Arabic know that this word can have different meanings, such as *going wrong* and *adding or deleting something*. It is worth noting that the Koran never says anything else about the Torah, only this word for Torah, which can have different meanings and interpretations. I think it would be much simpler if the Koran mentioned clearly that it is not the Torah that Gd wanted for humanity, to prove the idea of those people who do not believe in Torah On the other hand, the Koran has many beautiful descriptions about the Torah. It states clearly in Koran that Gd's orders are found in the Torah and Jews should obey them and there is also light in the Torah (reference 1). Obviously, all these verses in the Koran about the Torah can have different interpretations.

Some Muslim authorities have said that because the name of the Muslim prophet is not in the Torah, the Torah has been changed through history. The Koran mentions that Jews had been familiar with Muslim prophets from different sources, and it says that the name of the prophet can be found in the Torah. Jews could have had familiarity with the Muslim prophet from many other sources, and there is no reason to believe that the name of the prophet had been written in Moses' Torah. There is an expression that everything can be found in the Torah if you look for it. I have to emphasize that the Torah is only Moses' Torah, the part that was sent to the main prophet by Gd. In other words, if the Koran is talking about other parts of the Torah, this will not invalidate our theory and belief.

The most important principle of our theory is that there is no contradiction between the Torah and Koran. If someone can find any word or part of any stories in the Torah and Koran that can be contradictory automatically disprove our theory.

I believe that the Torah and the Koran come from the same root. Although there are different laws and orders in the Torah and the Koran, the Koran doesn't refute anything that the Torah mentions, and vice versa. Note that having different orders and laws for different nations is not strange. It is completely acceptable if Gd would have asked different things from different people and ordered them with different laws. If you see different laws in the Torah and the Koran, this is no reason to believe that these two books are contradicting each other. If you find two different stories about the same event or same prophet, then you can say that this is a contradiction, but as I mentioned before, there is no difference in the Torah or Koran about any part of history. This by itself can be the best proof that people can believe in both books and only a true belief can bring these two religions closer to each other. This belief not only makes peace between Islam and Judaism, but it also can bring all other religions closer to each other and bring peace among all the religions.

Now let us discuss Western philosophy and the Torah. The Western philosophers can generally be divided into two groups. The first group includes those who believe there was no Torah from the beginning. This group may not even believe in Gd, so we do not have to discuss this group that much. The second group consists of those philosophers who believe there was a Torah but that it has been changed, and what is left now is not the real Torah that Gd sent to Moses.

Before discussing these philosophers, I need to mention an interesting point. If someone believes in Gd and believes that the Torah has been sent from Gd to Moses and that this Torah has changed through the years, he should automatically believe in Gd. If he believes in Gd, he should believe in some kind of relationship between humanity and Gd. If he believes in the religion without the book and without the words of Gd, this kind of religion cannot be a true one. What I am trying to say is that these philosophers, even from the beginning, have some kind of self-contradiction in their beliefs.

In their books, they usually start with this: "We do not see any historical evidence about the Torah." They also see some differences between the Torah and science. In addition, and this is probably the main thing, they believe that there are differences between the parts of the Torah, and they don't believe that it could have been written by one person.

I do not think we need to talk about history and science, because what we have as history is incomplete. Even the history of the main events in the past has been lost completely, so lack of history or archaeological evidences of Torah cannot be a reason not to believe in it. The Torah was written in a symbolic language that can have many different interpretations. If something has been written in this language, it cannot be interpreted as a scientific book. We cannot compare science with the Torah. The Torah is not a science book and was never been meant to be. Whoever wants to find differences between the Torah and the sciences is wasting his time.

The other problem we see and hear about the Torah is what philosophers say about the differences among parts of the Torah. These differences have never been important in the past, until Western philosophers started talking about them. They say that the different parts of the Torah look different, and because they do, they should have different authors. This is an interesting point, but there is a simple answer for this. Maybe it was meant to be different from the beginning. We should know that almost all the differences that these philosophers have pointed out have been picked up by rabbinical authorities and have been explained in many books. We could write another book about this subject. We should not live based on assumptions of some philosophers, because these are all simply assumptions. As I mentioned in the preface of this book, these people are trying to build a life with assumptions that can never be proved. If there is a Gd, a Torah, and a way of living but somebody wants to disprove all these things, he should propose a good reason in order to do so. It is not enough to say that these philosophers have found things in the Torah that they cannot explain. Some of these philosophers do not even know the Hebrew language well.

Again, I did not put the Torah as the base of our discussion because of some doubts in the Torah, even though I think these are not true doubts. I picked up the Koran as the base for the book and theory, but as I mentioned, the Torah can be a strong help to the Koran. For those who believe in the Koran, we earlier discussed that there is no contradiction between the Torah and the Koran. If there is no contradiction between them, how can it be that there is contradiction in the Torah itself? For those who believe in Christianity, Jesus never mentioned that the Torah has changed.

Jews have been spread around the world for more than 2,500 years, but in spite of that, there is just one Torah, with minor differences in all the archeological discoveries. Again, what I mean by the Torah are the five books of Moses written in the Hebrew language. All the differences are in few letters, not even a word and with no changes in the meanings, and all these differences have been explained in different ways. In fact, these small differences are proof that despite large geographic distances between Jews in history, and under so many pressures, the Torah was kept faithfully, with minor unavoidable mistakes in writing and transmitting the traditions. There are many books of commentary from more than one to two thousand years ago, which all interpreted all aspects of the Torah. All these books are reasons to believe that the Torah is the same Torah that has been around at least for two thousand years, before the times of the New Testament and the Koran, and then, as we discussed, the Koran itself is the best proof for the Torah. I think that if people do not believe in the Torah, the main reason is the lack of knowledge about it. If they could study the Torah in depth, with all the interpretations, they would understand that the chances of there being any changes in the Torah are low.

I may not have an explanation for all the questions and difficult problems, but if we have to follow a theory in this world, we should follow one that would cover all the possibilities, as it would be closer to the truth. If we bring a theory to the world, it should be able to answer the questions in the world in a better way. The whole purpose is to bring us closer to the truth.

Now, after we talk about the Torah, we have to say some words about other books and other religions. Beside the Koran and Torah, the other prophets' books that are available in the world, even their own authorities believe that the books are not the same books that have been given to the prophets. What we are trying to determine at this point is how we can accept religions that have lost their words from the prophets.

About Christianity, there is a question that Gd has given any book like Torah or Koran to Jesus or not. What we have are books that were written after Jesus, and there is a question of whether Jesus himself wrote any book. If Jesus himself never wrote a book, the problem is easier to solve because if there was no book to begin with, then there is no problem that there is no book at present time, too. Then Christianity should use the Torah as a base for its beliefs because, for any religion, the base is the word of Gd to the prophet. The only thing we can follow is the word of Gd, which has been kept without any changes. The exact words of Gd are very important, especially the ones He used when he spoke to the prophets. There should be no translation or interpretation for these words. After the words of Gd have been given to the prophets, then other authorities can interpret the meaning of the words, but the first condition is to have the words from Gd. If Christianity does not accept the Torah as the word of Gd with no changes, then it will cut its own root.

Any religion in the world currently existing and believing in Gd believes that Gd talked to prophets and brought their religion to the world, so if they lost the words of Gd, they would have a problem. As we discussed in previous chapters, although these religions still exist and can be accepted, if a religion has lost the words of Gd, its basis cannot be very strong. This religion might encounter problems with its followers in the future.

There is a question of whether Jews can remain Jews and at the same time accept the other prophets. For example, can a Jew accept Jesus as a prophet of Gd, and at the same time, can a Christian accept Islam as a religion? This would be a problem because if a Jew accepted Jesus as a prophet, wouldn't he be obligated to change his religion? We answered this question briefly in previous chapters, but it bears repeating that if a prophet comes from Gd and proves himself to humanity, everyone is obligated to follow him and do as he says. There are two points to make. First, we currently do not have any reason to believe that any prophet ordered the followers of the previous religions to leave their religion and follow the new one. He might have suggested it to them, but the question is whether he put it as an order. These two are very different. He might ask them to believe in his prophecy and respect the new religion, but changing the old religion and coming to a new religion is something different.

Second, as we discussed in previous chapters, conversion per se cannot be obligatory unless the word of Gd is commanding the conversion. The fact is that at the present time, conversion is not the same as it was at the time of the prophets. Back then, there was a clear command from the prophets and Gd, but currently there is no clearance like before. Presently, all the religions claim that they are the best, and each religion has been divided into many branches. There is no clear way to choose any religion over the others. Any religion, as long as it follows the way of Gd and fulfills the criteria that we previously mentioned, can be accepted, but conversion to a new religion is different from accepting prophecy and the word of Gd.

In summary, if a Jew accepts Jesus as a prophet, it does not obligate him to convert to Christianity. Similarly, if a Christian accepts Islam as a religion that has come from Gd, he still can follow his own traditions.

The other question that may arise is why we should make ourselves so confused into the problem of religions. Isn't it confusing to accept all the religions and follow just one of them?

Isn't it better to find the best one and then encourage everyone to follow only one? As you can guess, this solution is almost impractical. People have tried in the past to do such a thing and it never happened, nor do I believe it will ever happen. The reason is in the problem of conversion. Even if it is possible to find one religion that is the best, we still have the other problem: that even the religions we think are best are not one religion anymore; they have been divided into branches. The differences between branches are much broader than the religions themselves. We should note that the religions have been different from the beginning, but the branches have been one religion and have been divided into branches. It means that maybe all the religions are right, but we cannot say all the branches are right. The branches have been created by the human mind, and out of all branches of one religion, there is just one branch that is right… or maybe none of them is right.

We should note that it is harder to find the right branch of one religion than it is to find the right religion. The question is, how can we find the right branch of any religion? This matter is completely dependent upon the authorities of the religions, and there is no way we can make peace between the authorities of one religion, because we are not part of that religion to begin with and we do not have the ability to make peace.

The other thing we should note is that even if we can find one branch of a religion, one that seems to be the best for everyone, the problem is not yet solved, because how can we be sure that all the laws and orders of this branch are 100 percent correct, even though other branches are not believing them. It seems there would be doubt in the human mind. If there is a doubt, we will still have the same problem that we have right now.

You might guess by now that the only way we can say which branches of the religions are right is to be guided by Gd. It means that the only way we will find the right way is if Gd tells us which one is right. Maybe that is the reason that in the whole history of humanity, man has been waiting for someone who is the final savior of the world, but until that time, we are obligated to live in the best way we can. Obviously, we are not closing the way to any religions or the branches of the religions. The road is open to everyone in every way. If any religion claims it is the best, it has to show and prove itself, and if people approve it, they will follow without doubt. Indeed, if we can make a connection among the religions, and they all respect the followers of other religions, there would be more opportunity to show what they have. We should open the way for all the religions and all the branches of the religions to live in peace and harmony with each other. We should respect any thought and encourage more research into it to find the right one. There is no problem in human life that man cannot find the solution for. If we go the right way, we can reach our goals much faster and with more confidence, and Gd will help us find the best way to Him.

Reference:

1. Koran, Al-Maedeh, 43-44

Chapter 7
UNITY AND DIFFERENCES

What we have discussed so far has brought us to the point that we need to have unity between religions. The whole purpose of having different religions in the world is to create and have unity between people of all kinds. We know as a principle that only through true unity can we solve the differences, and the more differences we can solve, the better unity we can have. In this chapter, I want to discuss a few more questions. First, what is our responsibility as far as obtaining unity? How can we solve our differences? If we solve our differences, then which religion or religions should humanity accept and respect? How does this theory of religions help make a better world? In the end, we will discuss this question: is there any other way in the world to attain this unity?

We can start from the basic question of how to obtain unity. The answer is not so hard. If all the religions of the world respect each other, listen to their ideas, try to see their problems as their own problems, and go to the roots of their problems, they will know each other better and live with each other better. Knowing each other is the first step in any kind of friendship. Without knowing each other, there won't be peace of any kind. Unfortunately, there have been such deep differences between the religions of the world, and we do not see much effort toward peace. While knowledge is the first step to peace, the second, and maybe the most important, step is the ability to understand the differences. It has become very difficult to obtain a true knowledge, without any personal preferences or preconceived ideas.

We should all know that without knowing each other we can never get to the point of knowing the world and knowing our creator. To know each other, we have to step forward and obtain enough knowledge of each other, and then we can have a healthy tolerance for different ideas. Not all the ideas are right, and not all the differences would be solved, but this would be the point of any discussion, book, or conference: to find the right and true ideology and to throw away all others that are based on anything other than true knowledge. At the same time, the only way we can find a true ideology is to have the tolerance to listen to each other and truly understand how someone can have an idea so different from us. That is the main purpose of this book—to create the opportunity for everyone to come and talk about his ideas. On the other hand, the religions also should avoid ideas that do not have any strong scientific or logical bases. I believe that if all the religions base their ideas, laws, and orders on a true base, which is accepted by all the religions and all the philosophers, then we can go further on this path to find true unity among all the religions. None of these dreams will come true unless we start knowing each other and attain more knowledge and faith.

As we discussed before, all religions are connected to each other like a chain, and if any of the rings become loose, it can affect all the other religions too. If you look at the books of those philosophers who do not believe in religion at all, you will see that they attack all the religions at the same time; this is because they do not believe in any concept that is above the physical world. In other words, the main purpose of religion is to give a true idea of the spiritual world and a true idea of Gd. I think the best proof for the Torah is the Koran because it repeats all the Torah's stories with small differences. If it were not for the Koran, it would be harder to believe even in Moses. If not for Judaism, Christianity would not exist, because the main basis of Christianity is Judaism. We are now living in a world where almost everyone has heard the name of Gd; this is because of all the different religions of the world. If you were living in a world where only a few people believed in Gd, you can imagine how difficult it would be to have any faith in Him.

Knowing each other and knowing different religions has another important aspect. This aspect of knowing each other comes when religions try to find the best way of living and start giving orders for life, For example, each religion has different ideas about the death penalty. At first glance, we can say no two of the religions have the same ideas, but if we look in detail, we can understand that all the religions are following a very basic fact, which is to have justice and mercy at the same time.

I do not mean that all the religions have the same ideas and the same orders in all aspects of life. What I mean is that if all religions try to listen to each other, they can have a better idea of how to solve the basic questions in the world. Because of this, not only can humanity have a better confidence in religion, but the followers of the religions will also feel more confident in themselves. Religions are like strings of different colors that should combine to make the best picture.

Maybe now we can understand why there are different religions to begin with. I think the main purpose of our creator in making different religions is to give us the ability to search and to solve the differences and, in the end, reach our own conclusions and find our own unity. It was not possible to create just one religion, because our minds did not have a correct concept of unity. All the religions have been divided into branches in the past. The main point is not that the ideology is right or wrong; because an ideology can correct itself by time provided that its follower are truly looking to find the right path. The followers of a religion should truly know the different concepts of a religion. This knowledge should not be colored with any prejudgment and personal desires. The less knowledgeable the followers of a religion are, the more branching will be happened to that religion. That is, if you see more branches in one religion, you can assume that more people in that religion are lacking a true knowledge of a religion.

The other important point we discussed in previous chapters is that although we need to know each other and obtain knowledge as much as we can from science and other ideas in the world, at the same time, we should not disqualify or refuse to follow a path that exists now. In other words, the way to find the right idea is to stay on our own way. If we lose our way, not only can we not understand the other ways in the world, but we are also going to lose what we have. True followers of truth should try to get knowledge of all the religions of the world, but they must follow one and only one way; otherwise, they will be lost in the big confusion of religions. The more we know each other, the more our ways of life become closer to each other, and that is the purpose of knowing each other—to make the gaps narrower. This is an important point that I need to emphasize. If someone is saying that none of the ways is right and that he is not going to follow any of them, it means that he will be lost in the end. There is no way that anyone finds the best way by himself. We should all be together and go together, but we should all stay in our own way. If somebody says that he follows his own way or that he follows all the religions as much as he can, it means that he is not following any of the right ways. And if that is the case, that he wants to follow his own way, not only is he not solving the problems, but he is also adding more problems because he is adding his own way. Any further branching in any religion by itself is a wrong way. Any branch that separates itself from the main pathway of the religion is a wrong pathway. The pathways to Gd are not that we can make, but Gd Himself made them. We just have to find the way he has shown. If we do not know any right way at this time, we should not make our own way to find Him.

My suggestion is that all the followers of all the religions should follow their own religions until a time comes that all humanity learns of a way that is known to be the best way. I do not mean that no one can convert to another religion, but I mean that no one can make his own way or make any changes. All of us should at least follow one of the existing ways. As we discussed in previous chapters, these ways should have a special criteria to be accepted as a religion.

Someone who truly believes in Gd is the one who follows Gd despite any loss that can potentially affect him. If we want to follow a religion, we are definitely going to lose some of our freedom and some enjoyment in the world, which in the beginning can be extremely difficult. We have to pay that price to find the right way. I believe that Gd will assist somebody who truly believes in Him with his whole heart and wants to find the best way to serve Him, but no one should make up his own way. I think this is currently one of the problems. People make their own religion. New groups come along, thinking they are right or can do better, but they do things that harm the whole future of humanity and the whole concept of religion. The more we go on our own way, the more we are separated and our unity is lost. The only solution to unity is trying to obtain common ground with others instead of making our own way.

In my opinion, the only one who can bring new laws is Gd Himself. He is the only one who can combine all the religions. He is the one who can make people follow any particular order. We cannot bring any specific law and ask people to follow us. What we can do is to obey what we have from our creator and follow his orders as much as we can. This is our job and responsibility, if we are looking for truth and peace. This way all the world's religions still exist and have different followers and the world would be in a better harmony that can make a unity much easier. I should say that if we do not learn the way to make a true unity, even if Gd brings just one religion to the world and asks everyone to follow this religion, we will eventually make branches out of this new religion, and will divide it to few religions. Humanity has to reach a much higher level of knowledge and wisdom in order to understand and respect other people's ideas and at the same time not lose ourselves in the ocean of confusion created by all these ideas. Any idea that is not based on a right knowledge and does not bring unity in the world is not a true and right idea. Those kinds of advertisements for any religion or any group can attract people for a while but will never give them a true and right concept of living, causing more harm for that group or religion—and humanity in the end.

Now let us ask a question that I think is one of the most popular questions on this subject. If someone does not feel a connection to any religion and thinks that living by religion is not the right way of living, what is this person supposed to do? What should he follow in life?

To answer this question, I need to bring you back to the beginning of this book. When we started to talk about religion, we began with one of the principle facts: we need to live in such a way that our consciences and our minds can be free of any doubt. There has been doubt in our lives, and there will always be doubt in what we are doing. This is the nature of living. This is the reason that humanity is still struggling to grow and the reason that many different ideologies are still existing. There is no way we can bring to the world a pathway that everyone will follow without question. There will always be questions and doubts on any pathway. We concluded that our responsibility is to live in such a way that we consider all the doubts and follow a certain way, one that allows us to live in peace with our consciences and minds.

Now let us go back to our question. If someone says that none of the world's religions is satisfying him, what is the answer? The answer is that everyone has the freedom to choose his way of life. No one can force anyone to follow a certain way. The only obligations we can put on another person are the obligations of society, the obligations that relate one to another. For example, we can punish someone for stealing, for killing, or for insulting, but we cannot punish someone for his ideology and for what he is thinking. By this, I mean that if someone wants to live in a certain way—as long as he respects others, does not interfere with someone else's way of life, and obeys the laws and orders of society—he is free. No one can ask him, for example, to pray, to fast, or to do certain things. He has the freedom of living, and no one can force him to obey any religion. Keeping faith and living on the basis of a religion is totally voluntary. The only way we can convince anybody to accept a certain rule is to make him think and doubt about his own believes, but he should have the freedom to choose between answering his conscience and obeying his desires.

The question is, if someone is conscientious and wants to find the best religion, what is he supposed to do? It is quite easy for someone to choose a religion, especially if this person has no background in any religion, but it will not be easy to find the best one. In my opinion, this is the positive aspect of all the religions and shows how all of them are connected and how they are similar in many aspects of life. I think, besides appearance, two religious persons from two different religions have much in common. On the other hand, we know that some of the religions are basic and simple, and some are comprehensive and advanced. The bottom line is that everyone has the responsibility to find the truth, to put away doubt from his life and follow the way of Gd. On this journey, no one should feel lonely. We should all move together. This way, without doubt, we will be able to answer all the questions soon.

Now let us look at the person who wants to keep a religion but none can satisfy him. In other words, he thinks all the religions of the world have lost their roots and connections to Gd. For a few reasons, this kind of opinion, as we discussed in previous chapters, cannot be right. What we said is that we are not the ones who make religion; Gd has created religions, and he has the responsibility of keeping them alive. Our responsibility is to find the pathways to Gd and to move on a certain path to get closer to Him. These pathways already exist.

Again, if there were no pathway, we would not have the obligation to find one. To clarify this point, I can say that the only reason we are religious is that there are religions in the world now. If there were no religions, no one had the obligation to go and make a certain pathway for him or certainly for a nation to get closer to Gd. Religions exist, and although we might have doubts in them, none of these doubts is enough to eliminate all the religions. If someone thinks all the religions have been going in the wrong direction, and there are no religions to choose from, that would be his choice of living., We cannot force anyone to follow any religion; this is between himself and Gd. All we can do is to present the Koran and the Torah to people, and the obligation falls on them to read and study with a pure heart and decide for themselves what to do. Choosing the right way and getting close to Gd certainly requires a pure heart and a pure mind.

In my opinion, that is the reason that Gd created different groups, different nations, and different religions. It is our responsibility to search and know each other. With this knowledge and understanding, we can go along a right path so that friendship replaces animosity and respect replaces war.

I would like to emphasize this point one more time. If someone thinks all the religions are wrong, or have been going wrong, this is his opinion, and he can live the way he wants to live, but no one can create any religion or any branch of religion. Creating a new religion is totally different from what we have been talking about in this book. To reiterate, we are not creating religions; they are already exist. No one can make a new religion or a new branch of any religion, certainly that would be the wrong way to go. If we have any obligations to obey any religion, that obligation comes from Gd for what He Himself has created.

As mentioned, I think there are religions in the world that keep the word of Gd. Our obligation is to find them and to live how Gd says. No one else can put any obligation on anyone and force him to go in a way that he thinks is right.

I should also remind that, nobody can interpret the existing religions in a way that he thinks is right. The authority to interpret religions has been put on the authorities of each religion, and needs certain qualifications that each religion has set for itself.

Now the question arises that if our theory is right, does it create more confusion or not? If we think all the religions are right, or some of them are right, and we should all respect each other with different ideas, then how can religions that are so different from each other exist without any conflict between them? I will give you an example.

Someone might ask, "If both the Koran and the Torah are right, isn't it right that we ask the Jewish clergy to learn about Islam and the Islamic clergy to learn about Judaism? If this were the case, what would happen if we found two completely different orders in these two religions? How can we find a common ground in a case where two religions have completely different ideas?

To answer these questions, I certainly think that there is no contradiction or contradictory words between the Torah and the Koran. I believe that the Koran and the Torah are confirming each other more than we can imagine. As I mentioned before, although the Torah and Koran are both the word of Gd, and there is no conflict of any source between them, it does not mean that Islam and Judaism have the same status. Gd, for a specific reason, has brought different religions to the world. These religions are different and have different orders. None of the religions is leaning on any other religion, and no one has the obligation to follow two different religions. In other words, there is no obligation for the clergy of any religion to master the other religions. Similarly, there should be enough knowledge of different religions so that when it comes to deciding about certain ways of living that might make a big difference in human life, the knowledge helps to choose the right way. I do not think there is any other way to find the right way of living. If we do not follow this way and limit ourselves to just one religion, we just cause more division of that religion at the end. Sometimes these branches will be so different from each other that each one will be like a totally new religion.

The reason for all the branching is lack of knowledge in the followers of that religion. The way of unity is not to go find the right way and force others to join. The way of unity is to understand that other people have different ways of thinking and living and understanding. We are all human, and we should know that if someone on the other side of the world is thinking differently from us, the reason is that he was born on the other side of the world.

Now I will discuss the last and probably the most important question. Am I picturing a religious society or not? What are we expecting from religions? How can we handle the freedom of living in a religious society?

The problem is that most religions do not currently give that much freedom to the people who don't like to obey the religion. Most of the religions do not allow the people to live freely and do what they like to do. Is this a mistake in religion or not? I can image that there will always be a group of people who will not live by any religion and will want to live freely, without any obligation of religion. Even in the best religious society, we can find this group of people, and they will always be living among religious people. How can they survive in a religious society?

Again, the whole purpose of interaction between religions is to get to the point of enough tolerance and understanding of the freely living. People of different religions have to come to this point to respect other people's way of living and ideas, even if those ideas are not religious ideas. Our lives and our world are totally dependent on our way of living and thinking. If we get to the point where we know how important it is to understand other people and their ideas, then we will reach the level of having a nearly perfect world. The question is, is there any other way to get to this point? Is there any other way that we can guarantee freedom for everyone in the world? Is there any other way that we can guarantee hope, prosperity, and a better life for everyone? I believe trying to understand and to know people causes a mutual respect. It starts from our minds and ideas, and it ends with our actions. Any society and any religion that cannot provide freedom will certainly not stay in the way of Gd. The way of Gd is giving freedom to humanity, allowing us to choose our way of living. Different religions have been brought to the world to give us the freedom to choose.

If the majority of the people in a society are religious, they should understand that being the majority by itself does not mean that they are right. They have rights as a majority, but minorities should have their own rights to live the way they wish, as long as they don't interfere with the way of life of the majority. On the other hand, if the majority of the society is not religious, they should provide enough support for religious groups. Each group should provide freedom of living for other people.

Can this book and these ideas guarantee this way of living? Certainly not. From the beginning of humanity until now, there are no guarantees in life, and there will never be any. Life is completely dependent on how we make the life for ourselves by learning, understanding and respecting each other.

I do not think that there is any other way that we can reach a point that true peace in all aspects of life can replace the fighting that exists in our world at this time.

Certainly, the only way we can guarantee this peace, harmony, and freedom is to provide enough knowledge for all groups of people, and each of these groups should try to understand and fully comprehend the meaning of living together in this world. I truly believe that religion can have an important role in this challenge. I do not think that without religions and without truly understanding our creation and future, we can reach a point that we understand each other and respect each other. That is the reason I started this book. We believe in Gd because we want to have a meaningful life, and if we need Gd to give meaning to this life, we need to follow his way, and if we want to follow his way, we have to understand and know all the ways that exist. True knowledge of the pathways of Gd is the final answer to our questions, and this kind of knowledge can certainly guarantee our freedom of living. This is the only way that shows us our future and shows the reward for following the right way and the punishment to those who follow their own way. No one has the right to decide what is wrong and what is right. The only thing we can say is that we have to come together to find the best way of living. If any of us wants to go his own way and make his own branch of living, he is certainly doing the wrong thing. We need two things: a scientific knowledge and a true faith. If we can have both true knowledge and true faith together, we will certainly be going the right way, but the guarantee still depends on ourselves. Certainly, in Gd we trust.

Chapter 8
CONCLUSION

The entire purpose of this book was to find a new way of looking at the world. As I mentioned in the beginning, no one can claim that he has answers to all the questions. The more answers we find, the more questions are raised. But I think this book offers a new way to look at and understand the problem. It at least brings me a little comfort that not all we are doing is worthless, and that one day, Gd willing, we will find answers to all the questions. If Gd helps us, we can go further, and if He wants, we will find more and more answers.

In the beginning of this book, I suggested that the whole reason we believe in Gd is to find the purpose of this world. If we do not believe in Gd, it automatically means that the purpose of the world is not known to us, and even if it is known, it does not make that much of a difference because we do not have any power to change it. Gd is the source of all goodness, and if we get close to Gd, we will improve ourselves. Finally, if there is no Gd, there will be no reward or punishment, and a world without reward and punishment will not last for long. Then we discussed the problem of religion.

Again, we do not make religions; we just follow them. If we believe in religion, this is not because we need religions. We follow religions because they exist in the world. As we discussed, it makes sense because if Gd exists, there should be a relationship between Him and humanity. That kind of relationship is religion. Religion is not just something about the past or present that we can make for ourselves; religion mostly deals with the future and that part of the human aspect that is not completely clear to us. We cannot see or touch that aspect of Gd, but we believe in it. That is the reason that humans cannot make religion for themselves. We can make any kind of ideology, but that ideology cannot be called a religion. Religion is simply something that has come from Gd and makes a connection between Gd and humanity.

Similarly, no one has the power to change an existing religion. If a religion changes from its original way, it cannot be called a religion any longer. Then we discussed that if we cannot make a religion and cannot understand a religion completely, it automatically means that we cannot differentiate between the religions. In other words, we do not have the ability to know which one of the religions is the best.

Although we cannot say which religion is right or wrong, we have the ability to find out which religion is true or false—by that, I mean a religion that came from Gd or was made by humans. A true religion is the kind that came from Gd and kept his word.

We mentioned some criteria for true religions, but differentiation of true and false religions is a hard task. In the history of humanity, the number of false religions and false prophets might outnumber the true religions and true prophets. In addition, as I said, it is almost impossible for humans to separate and recognize true religions on just the basis of our understanding. The way we suggested in this book was that we should consider them based on their documents which they have from Gd. The essence of any religion is the document from Gd. The document should be a book that has been sent by Gd to the main prophet of the religion, and those religions that do not have these complete documents cannot be independent religions by themselves. As discussed, if a religion has lost the main document of the prophet, it automatically cannot be relied on. If there are no documents and direct orders from Gd to give us guidance for living, then that religion cannot be a reliable ideology for us.

Currently, two religions in the world claim to have the original documents from Gd to the main prophet of the religion: Judaism and Islam. Other religions of the world either from beginning did not have clear documents from Gd to the prophet and were just followers of the other religions; or if they had any documents in the past, these have been lost or changed and the original documents do not exist anymore. Between Judaism and Islam, Islam has less doubt about the history of its documents. The Koran is the only book whose history, from the time of its prophecy, is clear to humanity.

As discussed, there are many similarities between the Koran and the Torah; there are no contradictions between the two. Although there are differences in the laws, the essence of both books is the same. The differences that might seem to be existed in the stories of prophets in Torah and Koran are easily explainable. I based my theory on these two books, clearly proposing the idea that these two books brought into the world two main religions that can complement each other.

We discussed that religions present at this time are not necessarily the same religions that were originated at the time of the prophets. Therefore, someone can believe in the Koran or the Torah, but it does not mean that he is accepting all other concepts of those religions. Likewise, no one has the right to make any religion by himself. No one can say that he follows this concept of religion but does not follow the other concepts. Each religion has its own totality that has been based on a basic concept, and this basic concept cannot be changed individually.

In short, we have accepted the Koran as the key to the religions. After the Koran, we discussed the other books and religions, and at the end, we suggested a new theory that basically brings all the religions into unity, in that all of them together are necessary for humanity to find the way to Gd. I emphasize again that we are not trying to make any new religion. The religions already exist. What we are trying to do is to find the common ground, that basic unity, among the religions.

Now we are discussing whether our theory is consistent with both the Koran and the Torah. This theory should not have any contradiction to what is written in both of them. Clearly in the Torah itself, we do not find any discussion about other religions. In the Talmud and other commentaries on Torah, we find very few comments about this topic, which make it very difficult to draw any conclusion. I leave this job to the Jewish scholars.

How about the Koran, does the Koran accept our theory? Is there anything in the Koran that is against our theory? In the entire Koran, we do not find any reason to contradict our theory. In the Koran, we can easily find the concept of unity between the people who believe in Gd (reference 1).

What is important is that the Koran does not negate our theory. If you look at the Koran, you will see that it is written clearly that those people from previous religions who believe in the Koran and their own book, will have rewards from Gd (reference 2). If you ask whether the Koran says that other books besides the Koran are complete, we can refer to the verse that says, "Torah is a complete book" (reference 3). Maybe more important than this is where it says, "Islam is the religion of Abraham," and in just the previous verse, the Koran is asking why we fight about Abraham—asking whether we know that Abraham was living before all the books in the world (reference 4).

All I am saying is that the Koran is not negating our theory; in many ways, it confirms it. Unity of the religions is possible, and the right religion is the religion of Abraham, a true religion, a religion beyond all other arguments and differences—a religion that came to us a long time before all other religions existed. We should all gather around the religion of Abraham and find the right way to get to our main goal, which is Gd. All this theory is doing, to find the way that we can gather around religion of Abraham.

One of the important problems that we discussed in detail, and which always arises as a big question and major argument, is what we should do with the differences in the laws among the religions. This is a general belief that when a religion comes, it automatically changes the previous laws. Even in the Koran it says that a new prophet can come and change the previous laws (reference 5). Each religion believes that because it has different laws, it is automatically different from other religions and calls itself better because of its unique laws.

What I wish to discuss further in this chapter is a basic question. Why has Gd brought different laws to different religions? Are the new laws more complete or better than the old laws? Even if the new laws are better, are we obliged to obey them, or they are optional? We discussed in previous chapters that it is difficult to answer these questions because it is difficult to say that some laws are better than others are. The second problem is that between now and the time of the prophets, many of the laws have changed for many reasons, and many religions now have different branches, each one with different laws. So it will not be simple to say that because of certain laws, this religion is preferred to others. Maybe these questions could have been answered much more easily at the time of the prophets, but currently we have to deal with this problem of religions in a different way.

As we discussed before, it is not logical to ask a person who is following certain laws to change his way of living almost 180 degrees. Even at the time of the prophets, it would not be logical to think that each prophet had asked the followers of the previous religion to completely forget about their religion and come to a new one. He could have suggested them, but to put an obligation for a person to change his religion and follow a new way of living, would have needed strong reasoning. The final word is that we do not find any verses in the Koran that obligate the followers of other religions to change to a new one. The Koran asks us to believe in the Koran, to follow the religion of Abraham and to obey Gd and his prophets. The Koran gives the reason for the diversity and different religions in the world (reference 6). It clearly states that all the religions should be unified to find the truth and follow the word, which is equal and the same among them (reference 7).

One of the other questions we have to answer, and which we tried to solve in previous chapters is this: if a religion has changed from its original form in different ways, what is our obligation to that religion? For sure, we are not obligated to follow a religion we know is wrong. Not only should we not follow it, but we should also try to discourage others from following it. If a religion has given off a few branches, does it mean that this religion has gone a different way than the prophet intended in the beginning? Essentially, I am saying that if a religion has new branches, how is it possible to say that all the branches are right? It is clear that when the religion began, there were no branches, and there was one law that Gd gave to the prophet. Now different branches of the religion have interpreted this law differently. In some aspects, the law completely changes between the branches of the same religions. So which one of these branches is right? Either one of them is right or all of them are wrong.

To answer this question, we looked at the religion from the beginning. The religions are a connection between humanity and Gd. We did not create any religions; they already existed. What we have to do is either accept or reject them. Because religions exist, it means that Gd has made a connection to us, and it means that we are obligated to get to Gd in certain ways. What we have now is a combination of different laws that have been gathered together in different religions. We as human beings have one obligation, and that is to follow the right way to Gd. We cannot make any new pathway for ourselves, because we do not know the ultimate goal of Gd in our life and creation. This pathway should have come from Gd to be accurate enough for us. In other words, we are not responsible for making a pathway, and we are not responsible for any damage done to the pathway of Gd. It is Gd's responsibility to keep at least one way clear and right to Him. It is our responsibility to find that way. If we know that something is wrong in any religion, we should not follow it, but if we have doubts, it does not mean that we should put it away.

The other point is that anyone can have his own ideas about religion and can follow what he thinks is right for him. We have the freedom to think, and this freedom will cause our growth in life. People should respect someone else's freedom to think and live in a way that is right for him; but we should know that we all grow together as a society, community, and a civilization.

Another question that comes to mind is why we cannot choose a religion, which is more reliable, make it a little more suitable for everyone and then encourage people to follow that religion. Isn't that a better way to find unity in this world? I am sure that you can guess that this is not possible for many reasons. The main reason is that we do not know which one is the best, and probably we will never come to an agreement about it. Another reason is that we do not have any authority to make any